T5-BAR-539

THE
COUNTRY AUCTION
ANTIQUES BOOK

THE COUNTRY AUCTION ANTIQUES BOOK

Cynthia and Julian Rockmore

Paintings and drawings by the authors

HAWTHORN BOOKS, INC.
Publishers / NEW YORK

THE COUNTRY AUCTION ANTIQUES BOOK

Copyright © 1974 by Cynthia and Julian Rockmore. Copyright under International and Pan-American Copyright Conventions. All rights reserved, including the right to reproduce this book or portions thereof in any form, except for the inclusion of brief quotations in a review. All inquiries should be addressed to Hawthorn Books, Inc., 260 Madison Avenue, New York, New York 10016. This book was manufactured in the United States of America and published simultaneously in Canada by Prentice-Hall of Canada, Limited, 1870 Birchmount Road, Scarborough, Ontario.

Library of Congress Catalog Card Number: 74-2572.

ISBN: 0-8015-1780-X

1 2 3 4 5 6 7 8 9 10

Contents

Introduction

Anyone who honestly believes that the opportunity to find and collect American antiques is over has not as yet attended his first country auction. Where auctions go on, antiques always appear, and where quantities of antiques exist, auctions inevitably take place. The two are practically inseparable. Auctions have become popular all over the country, because people enjoy searching for (and finding) bargains.

There are probably more American antiques changing hands at this time than at any former period in American history. Admittedly, prices are higher. But the same is true about everything else one buys. Oddly enough, in this case, the price increase is all to the good, simply because higher prices are an inducement to collectors to sell.

Collections of fine early pieces that might never have been available to the buyer in the open market are now appearing in the marketplace and at auctions. Collections are for sale because prices are right. And, in antiques circles, when a price is right for a seller, it is very likely to be equally opportune for a buyer. Collectors have a tendency to "trade up" their collections, and in our long experience, we have never seen good antiques go down in price. Time and care and the interest in antiques of ever-growing numbers of people have, of course, made them more costly and at the same time worth more—the simple rule of supply and demand. There is only an arbitrary increase in their price, but, because of limited supply, there is also an acknowledged increase in their value. This "recycling" of collections is a natural sequence of changing times. For collecting and collections belong, appropriately, to everyone.

In some cases, collectors pass their antiques along to relatives or friends, those pieces they prefer to keep in the "family." The balance is then usually sent to market to be converted into cash—often a surprising amount of cash, certainly a great deal more than the original purchase price. American antiques have more than tripled in value in the last few years, and those who have collected them have watched their value increase in an extraordinary manner. Antique collecting is a unique form of investing, for there is no charge for the usage or the prestige or the enjoyment of owning a collection.

People who learn about these furnishings made during our country's early times have come to love living with them, and it is very easy for anyone at whatever economic level to participate in the fun of antiquing. All it takes is a little study, interest in America, a bit of taste and judgment, and, lastly, the exciting experience of attending an auction or two. Then, you are on your own.

It is not necessary to plunge right in and bid your first day at an auction. The day spent in the country and the whole exciting new experience will in itself be worth the price of admission. To return home after an exhilarating day causes you to view your possessions in a completely new light. If there now appears to be some veneer peeling from one of your simulated mahogany pieces, it will very likely set you to wonder, as it did us a long time ago.

The tendency of the newly initiated bidder appearing at his first auction is to bid on everything, even objects he really doesn't want. The excitement that gets him caught up in the bidding, willy-nilly, is perfectly normal. Bidding usually starts very low, obviously much under the actual value, and the inexperienced are fearful of losing such a bargain and rush into the bidding. The very idea of being able, perhaps, to buy something, even if you don't want it, because it is so cheap, can become almost irresistible. That kind of urge to buy is strictly for dealers, for they are there to bid and buy anything, as long as the purchase price will allow them to resell the article at a profit. Sometimes a dealer has a particular buyer in mind and sometimes his purchase is speculative, but you can depend upon his motive being one of profit.

But you, the embryonic collector, are buying for your own needs and use and, whatever you buy, it must be something that you really want.

Garage sales are a way of disposing of the things people buy that they really don't want or, at best, articles in reasonably good repair that have outlived their usefulness. Antiques never fit into this category. If one becomes disenchanted with an antique, it is very simple to dispose of it. The marketplace is always ready to take it off his hands.

Part of our enjoyment over the years has been to spend leisure time looking at private and public collections whenever possible. Nothing is better than to go to the experts to look and learn. We started at the bottom of the antiques ladder, just like everyone else, furnishing our home with secondhand pieces bought in the backcountry auctions of Massachusetts and Pennsylvania where our minimal cash would stretch a bit further. More often than not, the pieces we bought needed refinishing or repair. We learned about that, too, first the hard way and then, thank goodness, we began to seek help from others. Libraries are chock-full of information on all subjects pertaining to American antiques and their care and feeding. One needs only the desire to learn.

The museums in metropolitan centers have fine collections of colonial artifacts. Some even have entire rooms decorated and furnished in the precise period of their original manufacture and use. We do not want you to believe that this "purist" kind of collecting or decorating is the preferred method. It looks great in the archives of a museum but not necessarily in our homes.

It is our recommendation to mix and match the furnishings of different periods. We believe that good pieces of American antiques, whatever their period, can live comfortably in context with the most modern of settings or vice versa. There is probably nothing so modern in the design sense of the word as some of our most primitive colonial furnishings. Just remember that they were also designed to be totally functional —a prime objective in the designing of modern furnishings.

Certainly fine glass, whether pressed or blown, patterned or overlay, graces any surroundings. The color and elegance of design, as well as the historic value of an art form add much to any room, regardless of its period.

Ironstone china, which incidentally is still being manufactured, will always have that most modern quality in its stark whiteness, regardless of the raised portions that distinguish its patterns. Any small piece of fine Americana will hold its own as a piece of artistry, whether alone or in a room of unassociated or similar decor. We hope that you select and purchase one good piece of Americana and place it in your home. We are certain that you will immediately become aware of the pleasures of collecting. We also recommend that you personally seek out and hunt down the things you want to buy, for we believe in the old Yankee expression, "If you cut your own wood, it will warm you twice."

This kind of thinking will also keep your interest in the subject a broad one, and make it a lot more fun. You will not have to pay the high costs of the competitive collecting of rare pieces. There is time enough for this later. To collect some expensive things when you can afford them, some less costly when you must, gives you options. Later, you may decide to keep collecting in one single kind or period and discard all the rest. It's up to you.

There are, however, some who have always collected the hard way, accumulating rare items of Americana that would have been costly and difficult to collect at the time they were made. For instance, American pewter was not made in as great a quantity as its European counterpart, and very few American pewter artifacts have survived. American silver suffered a similar fate. Wealthy colonials who collected silver for both decorative and monetary reasons followed the fashion of the times and sent their colonial silver to be melted down and restyled by the then more popular English silversmiths. There are, however, some great collections of colonial silver in this country, including those of Judge Alphonso T. Clearwater and Mabel Brady and Francis P. Garvin. It behooves a newly beginning collector to pause and consider, at least on the subject of collecting American silver, regardless of his enthusiasm for the subject and/or regardless of his financial resources.

With the large choice of Americana flooding the country through the early and late Victorian times and continuing on up through the turn of the century, there are ample directions and objects to interest anyone who has the desire to collect.

Each person collects Americana for a variety of reasons. We cannot help but believe, regardless of the size or value of these collections, that the original and most important motivation is love of beautiful man-made things.

Americans are about to celebrate the two-hundredth anniversary of our country's history. Much attention will direct itself to those artifacts that have represented its progress through two centuries of art and growth.

Sugar Bush
Farm Auction
in Salem

There is perhaps no place in the whole world quite as beautiful as New England in the autumn with the ochres and golden yellows of the maple leaves playing their light and color against the deep red of the oaks. The air is as exhilarating as wine. To take off for an auction in the Berkshires at this time of year is a privilege.

The narrow road we entered to reach the auction at Sugar Bush Farm led off from the charming little town of Salem. Its typical little common with the prettiest of Oliver Wren churches at the end was flanked by a fine New England meetinghouse with a picket fence and gate. The white clapboard houses all seemed spanking clean against the crisp blue of the sky. The road we took was first a narrow blacktop. It ended abruptly and became a deep-rutted dirt road that quickly became grassed over in the center as we went along, until the ruts were hardly visible from lack of use. The road must have been used solely by the farm at the end of the road, for stone walls and maple trees on both sides of us seemed to be closing in. The gaps between the walls and trees revealed fields in long disuse, with tall weeds covering rock-strewn slopes.

As we entered the clearing in front of the house, the road we were traveling appeared to go every which way—to the barns, the sheds, the sugar house, and the dwelling. There apparently had never been a formal garden; flowers were planted along the stone walls. The scene had the look of a New England farm that had been abandoned, yet at the same time was lived in. It is not that New Englanders do not care about their farms, but operating farms in New England is difficult. What with the shortest growing seasons, frost as early as September and often as late in the spring as May, only the hardiest of plants, or people for that matter, can survive. The cold in the winter makes the heating of these wooden houses difficult, and the winter wind pushes drifting snow through cracks in walls one wouldn't know existed.

This particular house was not one of the earliest; its lines were not classic. It looked as though it had never been painted, but it had the beauty of a lived-in, working home, the same kind of impressive look that its family must have had.

Lying low in the valley below new highway construction, this farm was doomed to find itself hundreds of feet under water. For this was the site of a recently completed dam for a new reservoir that would supply water to the city of Boston, some eighty miles to the east. Everything was to be sold except the land, of course. Even the trees would be cut and milled or corded. The house would be torn down, its lumber sold, and what was left would be burned.

The crowd assembled at this farm was fairly large and mainly local. We knew that the auction would start on time, for there is something uncannily punctual about New Englanders. Perhaps it is the weather that trains them never to put things off.

The inside of the house was warm and stuffy; characteristically, the windows were not open and had the look of never having been opened. One of the iron lids on the kitchen range was tipped to reveal the glowing blue flame fed from the chunk wood in the firebox. A big oak drop leaf table was piled high with small things to be sold, and my companion wasted no time in inspecting them. New England is pressed-glass country, and it is still possible to find rare bits and fine pieces that have survived the times and daily usage.

Early pewter is another possible find in out-of-the-way auctions, the kind of American pewter that largely disappeared during the War of Independence. Patriots at that time melted down their pewter to supply the colonial army with shot for their rifles. Pewter, heavy with tin, originally filled the taverns and public places of the more populous towns of New England, but eventually many heavy mugs and plates were sent into service for freedom. In the areas of the backcountry, however, the quantity of this early Americana was small, and the War for Independence was not as close. Sometimes select pieces of early design and fine quality pewter remain in cupboards and on shelves where they were placed many years before.

The poorer farms in backcountry areas of New England were not the kinds of places where decorating changes took place. Fashions that influenced homemakers of coastal towns rarely reached the inland areas. These areas, at the same time, had very little commerce or communication with the world outside of their immediate surroundings. Glass, clocks, and early brass did find their way into these remote areas through the traders and general stores. Much of the valuable glass, particularly Sandwich glass, was packaged as premium items. Sandwich, one of the first kinds of glass to be manufactured mechanically and in great quantities, had very little status originally. But as abundant as it originally was, it was bound to become rare. However, we found ourselves a place where unusual pieces of pressed glass could be found. It seemed as if each early antique was lying where it had been placed many years before. We knew we were romanticizing, for the house had not been abandoned that long; it just gave a long-unused impression.

We were hoping to find a wall clock. A clock would have been a necessity for a farm so far from Salem. Clocks, it seems to us, are New England, and an important part of its history. With names like Seth Thomas, Elias Ingraham, Simon Willard, and his brother Aaron Willard, all from Connecticut and Massachusetts—it did not seem unheard of to find a rare timepiece. Clocks were carefully used. Clocks were ageless. Clocks were likely to be cared for as if they were members of a family. Clocks were one of the few mechanically operated articles in entire households. They gave information and needed little attention other than winding. Clocks lasted forever in households for all these reasons, in addition to the fact that generally they were placed in the safest of places, usually on a mantel over a fireplace or hung high on a wall away from where hazardous action would occur. Clocks often were given as wedding gifts and cherished for entire lifetimes. Although a house's furnishings, indeed, the house itself, might be plain, fine, gay, and extravagant clocks often are found, perhaps the gifts of loving ones, years before. More often than not, the gift of a clock was out of context with the economic condition of both the giver and the receiver. And, if one reads periodicals of the late 1700s or early 1800s, one discovers that early in the history of the colonies clocks were well on their way to becoming most desirable and practical home essentials. Clocks were the status symbol of their time. And, their sales closely followed those of early lighting fixtures.

Lamps, we thought, were bound to be found in this kind of auction, for electricity would be a recent addition to this out-of-the-way household. The electric supply leading into this house—a two-wire affair—indicated its maximum 100-volt capacity. It was located at the end of a road and was the last in line of an electrical supply. This all added up to the possibility of a need in this house for alternative lighting. In any case, the small incandescent bulb hanging from the center of the kitchen ceiling would not be capable of giving much more light than a clean chimney and a well-trimmed wick in a kerosene lamp. Certainly its light could not compete with a Rayo lamp of the gas-mantle type. Lamps had to be there all right, and they were: wall-bracket types and hanging lamps—one with a particularly attractive painted glass shade. Not a bold painting on its surface, but delicate flower and fern designs, which looked more like a Japanese painting than the usual designs that are found on Victorian milk glass lamp shades. There were no prisms hanging from it. There may never have been any, although the tiny holes for the hanging wires were there in the metal ring that held the shade. People in those early days bought lamps a piece at a time—the kerosene font, the frame, the shade, the decorative brasses, even the burners were interchangeable. It gave the buyer a choice of light—single narrow wick or large double wick—as well as a choice of utilitarian or decorative lamp. It was much like a decision to purchase a four-cylinder car or a V-eight, which depends upon one's ego and on how much gas or mileage one desires or can afford.

The auction began to move along in the yard, with the selling of farm tools, rusted farm equipment, and piles of lumber. Many of the bidders appeared to be neighbors. Their main interest was the farm equipment. It took a while for us to acclimate ourselves and our hearing to the pace of the sale. The accent of the auctioneer was no help, nor was the speed with which he talked. He told the usual number of jokes, none of which sounded funny to us, although the local people seemed to enjoy them. Joking seems to be an absolute compulsion for most auctioneers, and it is difficult to know whether the people laugh at the joke or the humorist. In any case, the sale was on its way.

It was efficiently run, oddly enough, and little time was wasted. It was understandable, for the light would not last long that short fall day, and everyone, including those conducting the sale, appeared to want to finish with it and get home for an early supper.

As we drove home at the end of the day, our station wagon filled with lots of purchases and a few very good buys, we had that wonderful feeling of a beautiful day well spent.

The purchases were not quite the same as our buys at an auction near Royalston Centre, a few miles north of Orange and Athol, Massachusetts. That was a truly different kind of day—but then every auction is expected to be different. That was a day of tent beds, drop leaf cherry tables, and the rarest of early pumpkin pine pieces. It was one of those most unusual events, that of a dealer's private collection going up for sale. It is all part of nature's recycling of antiques. Dealers and collectors also pass away, and more often than not the heirs are less interested in the collections than they are in the cash that the pieces will bring. Offers to them for individual pieces at ever-increasing prices, normally lead heirs to open their auctions to the public.

The Royalston sale was a spectacular one, and the prices paid were high. Our education at the marketplace was well worth the day, although we spent a bit more of our meager cash reserve than we could or should have. In retrospect, of course, we should have bought the whole sale out, even though we couldn't possibly have afforded to do so.

The few short years since have seen the value of most of the items sold increase four or five times the original auction prices. Unhappily, we kept a record of the pieces we wanted and the price they were bought for that day, and those records are covered with tears from the very eyes that did not see into the future.

We all spend a major part of our lives in our homes, and our furnishings are a formative part of our environment. We all feel pride in the beginnings of this country and in the people who made it work, and antiques serve as important visual reminders of our impressive past. If we look around us, we see many articles of modern manufacture that imitate the classic designs of colonial times. Plastic manufacturers work very hard to simulate wood textures of pine and walnut. The significance of this is obvious.

Fortunately for all of us, antiques are here to stay. Each period of history produces several pieces that time and survival will designate as genuine Americana. There are probably just as many fine things made today that will eventually belong in this category. Your enjoyment of the Americana of the 1700s and 1800s will help you to find the Americana of today.

Top left: Mahogany corner cupboard built to display fine china. Tasteful carvings are reminiscent of built-in corner cupboards of finer homes of the early 1800s. "H" hinges are of brass.

Top right: The delicate turnings in the middle back of this Windsor chair and the "H" brace added very little to the comfort of this attractive chair. 1765–1800.

Bottom left: Silver teapot with unusual ball feet. W. G. Forbes, 1805. Teapots of this style were made in pewter as well as silver. The handle was generally of wood or horn to eliminate the heat on the handle.

Bottom right: Brass-handled fireplace shovel and tongs. Often the design of these pieces was an adaptation of the pattern of the andirons and were made in sets, often designed along with the firerail or fender.

16

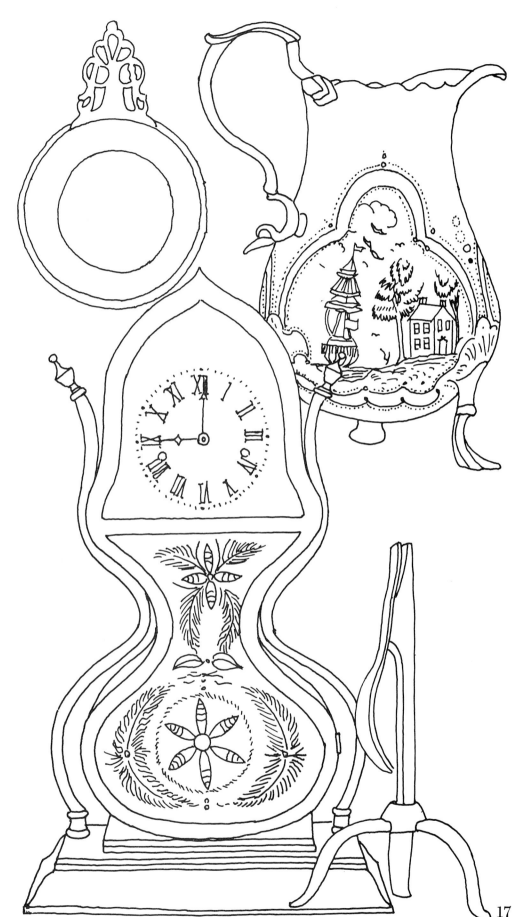

Top left: Porringer by William Holmes, Sr., nephew of Benjamin Franklin. This silver convex-sided bowl has a graceful cinquefoil-pattern "keyhole" handle. Massachusetts, late eighteenth century.

Top right: Silver milk server. The engraving by Nathaniel Hurd is of the owner's ship and home. Boston, 1750s. It was not uncommon for artisans to make or decorate articles to order.

Bottom left: Eight-day acorn mantel clock. This fantastic clock is one of the most sought-after clocks by collectors. Forestville Manufacturing Company, Connecticut, 1850.

Bottom right: Rush light holder of wrought iron. An extremely primitive piece. Probably New England, early eighteenth century.

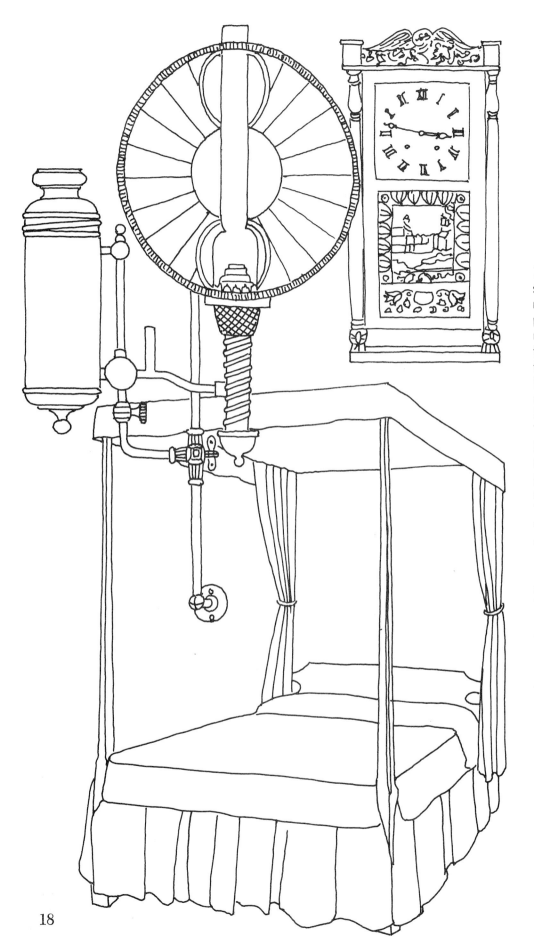

Top left: Perfection student lamp with mirrored reflector, patented 1881. The multiple adjustments that can be made on this wall lamp to direct light to any given spot made it a most popular light for barbershops. The kerosene font is blue pressed glass with self-operating spring plunger to feed kerosene to wick as needed. The small round wick is very efficient. (Authors' collection)

Top right: Eight-day-movement wall clock. The decal on top piece is of an eagle, and the painted glass depicts a New England common. Early New England, attributed to Eli Terry and Sons, Clockmakers.

Bottom: Colonial eight-sided posts. Their plain contour indicates that they were made to be covered with the closed drapes. This bed is typical of the period when the head of the bed was still draped and the foot clear of either drapes or wood construction.

18

Top right: Primitive hanging corner cupboard. Beveled door panels, strap hinges. New England, 1790s.

Top left: Three-back waved-comb Windsor chair. Middle eighteenth century.

Center: Maple and pine butterfly table. New England, 1710–1740.

Center left: H. L. Brewster and Company shelf clock. Bristol, Connecticut, 1860.

Center right: Blown three-mold sugar bowl and cover. New England, circa 1830.

Bottom right: Heavy tin candle mold, handle and base of wrought iron. Mold is for ten candles.

Bottom left: Pine reel for measuring and skeining yarn. The box behind the hub of the wheel is geared to release a clapper, indicating that a full skein has been gathered.

19

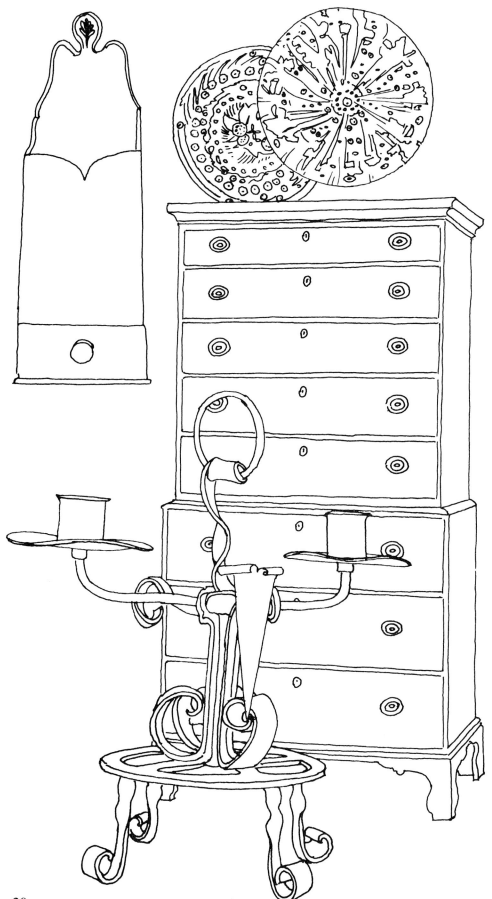

Top left: Carved-top one-drawer pipe rack. Drawer is for tobacco.

Top right: Two American paperweights. These beautiful pieces were created by many American glass companies: Sandwich, Gilliland, New England Glass Company. There were also some important pieces of fine French manufacture shipped into the States prior to 1850.

Center: New England maple chest-on-chest. Stamped brass fittings and graduated drawers. Keyholes are decorative only. Normally a lock was placed only in the top drawer. Middle eighteenth century.

Bottom: Intricate table sconce. Wrought iron, designed with ring carrier handle and attached candle snuffer. This rather extravagant piece of forging indicates a late period where little attention was paid to lack of material by the blacksmith.

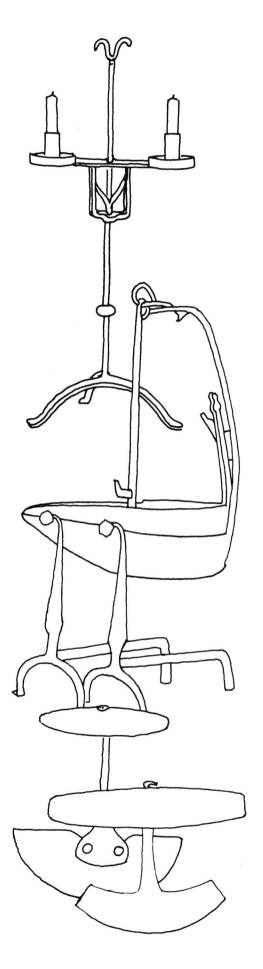

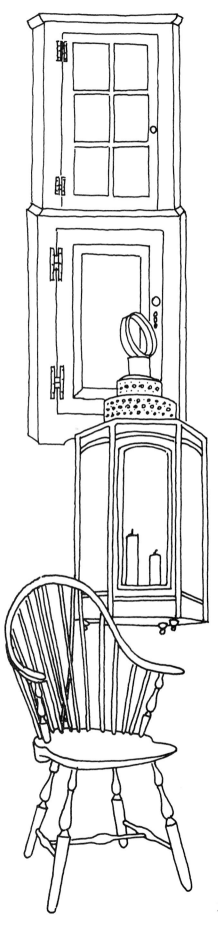

Top left: Wrought-iron candlestand with adjustable arm for two candles. Early eighteenth century.

Upper left center: The wrought-iron Betty lamp shown is one of the earliest types although Betty lamps were in use and manufactured continuously through the eighteenth century up until the late nineteenth century.

Lower left center: Wrought-iron andirons said to have been made in Salisbury, Connecticut. Most of this type of forging was done by local blacksmiths.

Bottom left: Two wrought-iron food choppers, both with whittled pine handles.

Top right: Early pine corner cabinet. Wrought-iron "H" hinges. Central New England.

Center right: Tin lantern, six-sided, glass panels, two candles. A four-sided lamp like this is believed to have signaled Paul Revere from Christ Church steeple in 1775.

Bottom right: Braced arch-back Windsor. Single bent piece for arms and back, turned "H" stretchers.

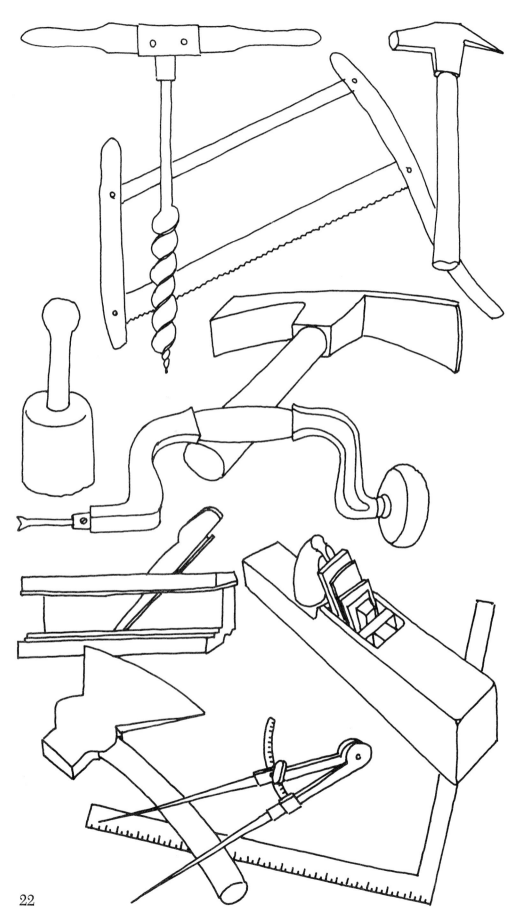

Principal tools of the carpenter include: auger, bucksaw, claw hammer, mallet for chisel work, brace and bit, adze, molding plane, jack plane or black plane, hatchet, compass for both dividers and circles, "square." These can be identified by reading left to right from the top.

There has been little or no change in tools for woodworking in two centuries, except modernization of individual items. As long as manpower was the only energy, attention was paid to the parts that were handheld. Little else improved in the simplest matters of leverage or gearing to ease the work load.

Even when water power became available, the tools the water drove were basically the same as the most primitive of hand tools. They were simply made larger.

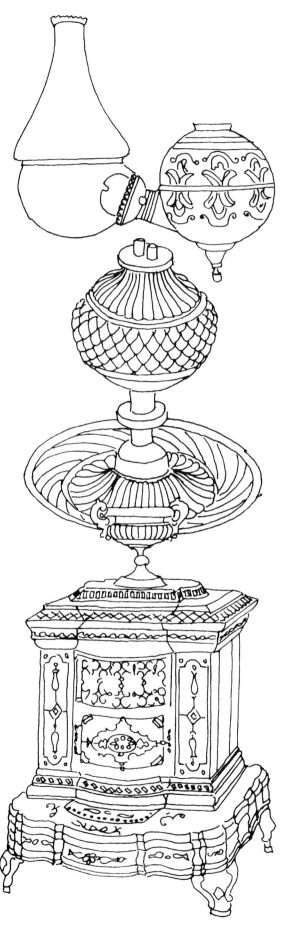

Top left: Angle lamp with clear glass base and opaque glass shade and chimney. Fuel oil reserve is of pressed brass. 1875.

Center left: Blown in three-piece mold with saucer base, this early whale-oil lamp is a rare item, indeed. New England, 1815–1840.

Bottom left: Decorative stoves like this were made in foundries in Albany, Buffalo, Baltimore, Pittsburgh, Boston, New York, and New Orleans. 1840–1875.

Top right: Open-top corner cabinet with serpentine framing in the Queen Anne style. Single paneled door is fitted with butterfly hinges. Shell design at top is typical of period.

Bottom near right: Parlor lamp, painted porcelain shade and base, brass font, and cast brass base. This style of lamp is often referred to as a "Gone with the Wind" lamp. Late Victorian.

Bottom far right: Brass urn-top andirons with forged-iron feet. Eighteenth century.

Top left: Ship lantern in lighthouse style. Brass case, heavy glass windows.

Bottom left: Empire music stand. Hexagon post, mahogany veneer. Music was, of course, a very special thing and those who practiced it naturally had everything made to their order. This charming stand is an elegant example.

Top right: Stanley's #1 chunk-wood stove. The double stovepipe that continues into an additional iron casting adds much to the efficiency of this parlor heating stove. These decorative stoves were made throughout New England and Pennsylvania in the middle 1800s.

Bottom right: Unusual trestle table. Single central post with identical turning of end posts. Very early eighteenth century.

24

Top left: Octagon stretcher table. A rare shape top of pine makes this rather unusual. Base and stretchers of maple. Early 1800s.

Center left: School-master's desk with stretcher base. Maple. Early eighteenth century.

Bottom left: Blown three-mold lamp with saucer base. Whale oil burner. New England, 1820–1840.

Top right: Shelf clock with kidney dial said to have been made by Benjamin Morel of New Hampshire, 1820–1830.

Center right: Large sapphire-blue sugar bowl and cover of Stiegel type in expanded diamond design. (Brooklyn Museum)

Bottom right: Blown three-mold pitcher in geometric pattern. Attributed to Boston and Sandwich Glass Company. Early eigh- teenth century.

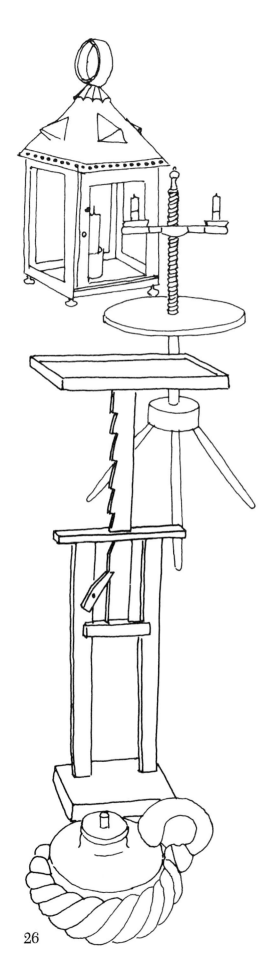

Top left: Blown-glass candle lamps or lanterns with heavy tin bases and tops. 1775–1820.

Center left: Two early New England adjustable light stands, top with screw adjustment and lower with ratchet adjustment. Primitive.

Bottom left: Blown three-mold sparking lamp. Sandwich, 1875. Lamps of this style were also made much earlier.

Top right: Square tin lanterns with gable-type ventilation and small cast-iron feet.

Center right: Salt glazed earthenware jar with cow motif. (Landis Valley Museum) These salt glazed preserving jars were made throughout New England and Pennsylvania.

Bottom right: Ship's lantern with reflector or magnifying glass chimney.

The Auction
Near the
Railroad Bridge
in Poughkeepsie

The Indians fishing the tributary stream above Kaal Rock could feel their canoes drifting gradually downstream toward the juncture of the Winnikee and the broad river that flowed to the sea. When the wind blew fiercely, they would leave the shoals teeming with fish and paddle their bark canoes to the safety of the harbor of Apokeepsinck.

More than fifty years after the first white men settled near this beautiful mountain-bordered river, a cockleshell of a ship, the *Half Moon*, bore Hendrick Hudson and his crew up the broad river to the mouth of the Winnikee.

The Dutch, true to their traditions, were great seekers after commerce, but they manifested little interest in settling the lands they found so far from their home ports. They traded in materials that they had transported in the holds of their ships. They purchased great tracts of land, in order to establish trading centers that would bring them profit with as little physical effort on their part as possible. The morality or legality of their purchases was never questioned, for the lands they found in this western world seemed limitless, and the Indians from whom they bought the land were easy to persuade. The Indians might have rationalized that the land traded away would never be settled or its primeval look destroyed by its new owners.

Not too long after the Dutch traders had opened up this part of the New World, these lands were transferred through war and attrition to the English. In or about 1664, titles or established legal rights became a part of every transfer of great tracts of land in the New World. It is stated in a historical record in the Duchess County Archives that, about 1682, a license to purchase a large tract of land was drawn up—a contractual agreement by the Dutch to buy the land from the Indians. The purchase was to encompass areas that were to become the towns of Fishkill and Wappinger, as well as major parts of La Grange and Poughkeepsie.

This early and important purchase of land in the Hudson River valley totaled some eighty-five thousand acres. Interestingly, a record of the price paid to the Indians by the Dutch was also recorded. The transfer included "Six bushels of winter wheat every year [it did not state, however, for how many years], One hundred Royalls, One hundred pound powder, Two hundred fathom white wampum, One hundred bars of lead, One hundred fathom of black wampum, Thirty tobacco boxes, Ten Holl edges, Thirty Gunns, Twenty blankets, Forty fathom of stroudwater cloth, Thirty Kettles, Forty Hatchets, Forty Hornes, Shirts, Stockings, Coats, Drawing Knives, Juggs, Bottles, Fouer Ankers of Rum, Ten Fatts of Beere and eighty pounds of tobacco." Surely a tremendous price to pay at that time for this undeveloped country, accessible only by water. The Indians who bargained away this land were to see its resale into smaller parcels at larger profits, and also to see the settling of the area begin.

The growth of that part of the Hudson Valley was relatively slow. Records disclose that the taxable inhabitants by the year 1771 numbered only 235. After that the population jumped to 2,529, a 1,000 percent increase by 1790, a short twenty years later.

On the seventh of January 1778, the Continental Convention assembled at Poughkeepsie, the first capital of the state, and the most noteworthy act of this meeting was to ratify the federal Constitution. Twenty-one years later, on March 27, 1799, Poughkeepsie was incorporated as a village, and by 1805 the village population had grown to a taxable list of 368 names, with real and personal property, it was noted, valued at over $400,000.

Two years later, in 1807, Robert Fulton's steamboat was making scheduled trips from Albany to New York and back, with stops along the Hudson. The seventeen-hour trip from Albany to Poughkeepsie was an important part of its schedule and the fare to that destination was quoted at four dollars.

Leon Kross, a well-to-do seaman and former master of his own ship, moved from Massachusetts and settled in the area. It was his dream that Poughkeepsie, with its entry to the sea and its proximity to the large markets of the East, could become an ideal place for a whaling port, one that might rival the port of New Bedford. The stone home he built close to the river was eventually to house a fine collection of antiques from that part of America. Not only had he brought his family and his entire worldly wealth to Poughkeepsie, but also his dreams and energy.

In 1830 the Poughkeepsie Whaling Company was formed. Friends of Kross, who also agreed that the area, in spite of its distance from the sea, would be ideal for the whaling industry, established a second group called the Dutch Whaling Company. Within two or three years, these companies proved to be failures, but undaunted, the enterprising Mr.

Kross turned his energy and attention to the manufacture of glass, an operation that also failed. His defunct glass business passed to his heirs and they sold it for whatever could be salvaged, and along with it a section of land to be used for the footings of a bridge to be built across the Hudson River, the bridge by which the South Mountain and Boston Railroad from New England later gained access to the coal, iron, and slate regions of Pennsylvania. Of the twenty-four spans holding the bridge, three were built on the land the Kross heirs had sold.

By 1889 the bridge was completed, a magnificent construction 2,608 feet long and over 200 feet high over the Hudson. The span dwarfed the Kross house, which was approximately 600 feet from the easternmost pier. Kross's son Adam spent his later years watching the trains on the high tracks moving great cargoes of freight to the east and to the west across the Hudson.

Roads along the river had improved greatly. Traffic, both north to Albany and Troy and south to New York City, passed Kross's large stone house. By virtue of the traffic, as well as proximity to the river's piers and the boats that carried people and cargo, the Kross home became an inn for the traveler and a secondhand store for the local area. The rather poor fare the inn was capable of serving brought the inn and food traffic to an end by popular demand. However, the secondhand business continued for many years. As the town prospered, better houses were built high on the hill. The riverbank area became less and less desirable, and the Kross property deteriorated both in appearance and value.

The building of Vassar College did not help this trend. Matthew Vassar, the wealthy and childless philanthropist, turned over 200 acres to the college he founded in 1861. Dedicated as he was to the idea of building a place of education for women, it was endowed with his contribution of $275,000 and equipped with buildings (built then for a cost of over half a million dollars). Matthew Vassar, Jr. and John Jay Vassar, nephews of Matthew Vassar, further endowed the school with $130,000.

The geographical direction of the educational and residential improvements of Poughkeepsie were again turned from the river's banks. Industry or business directed to warehousing further depressed the waterfront area. It was only a matter of time before the Kross land was used for smaller and less important business. And so it declined in value for years until, for reasons of extreme necessity, what property was left was put up for auction to satisfy taxes and debts.

The contents of the house were a hodgepodge of periods, for the elder Kross and his son Adam had both experienced wealth and failure. The furnishings were in varying states of disrepair, but because of its early history, the house was bound to reveal some remarkable pieces of early Americana.

Few people had set foot in Kross's house, or even on his property, for that matter, in the last few years. Rumor had it that the accumulation of bric-a-brac and furnishings included many priceless pieces from the early whaling days. It all remained to be seen, however, for the wily old gentleman was not about to allow the usual preinspection of his home or its contents. Had he been able to accomplish it, each piece, as it was to be displayed to the buyers assembled there, would have been as much a surprise to the auctioneer as it would have been to the bidder. This rather unorthodox procedure would have been followed simply out of respect to the wishes of the old gentleman. But, unhappily for him, legal pressures were brought to bear and the auction, along with its preview of the contents of the house, proceeded along more conventional lines. It might be added that the notoriety caused by the legal hassle over the court's procedure drew a considerably larger audience than it might have had had the sale just been advertised in the usual way. In any case, it added even more of a treasure-hunt aspect to the event.

The house was so jam-packed with things, it was hard to believe. Old Mr. Kross had outdone his father in the practice of never throwing anything away. There were articles representing the periods from the very day the house was completed and originally furnished in 1820. Apparently nothing had ever been discarded. It was a virtual storehouse of antiques and memorabilia from a century and a half of American history. There was bright bloodred ruby overlay of the kind found only in New England and small bits of pewter mixed in with odd sherry glasses made of the earliest of flint glass.

Another curious aspect of the material was a result of the background of the original builder. Kross's father's first love had been the sea. His early youth had been spent along the New England coast. It was only natural that he had brought with him, when establishing his new life on the Hudson, many of the artifacts of that Atlantic area, articles seen only in auctions that might have taken place in New England seaports, such as Rockport or Martha's Vineyard. For instance, a fine collection of scrimshaw came to light. Packed in a case in one of the upper rooms, a valuable sea chest and its contents had all the appearance of never having been opened. The pieces of walrus and whalebone seemed to have been packed as soon as the sailors who had made them arrived in port, never again in the next 150 years to be brought to light until this final auction of all the belongings of the household.

The articles that were in perfect condition were of great value; unfortunately, a great many of the objects were cracked or chipped. The variety of the pieces, as well as their general condition, were a reminder of the long period during which the house served as a secondhand store. Very few of the pieces had been moved about over the years, so they had undoubtedly been purchased in a damaged condition. Had everything been in mint condition, the pieces would have been priceless.

As the day wore on, it was obvious that the auction would take the two days as advertised, for the bidding, even for the chipped pieces, was "salty." It seemed as though everyone in Poughkeepsie wanted something from this ancient house. It was also apparent that the damaged articles would not discourage the bidding. Admittedly, we also have been guilty of this same bad habit—buying what collectors call a shelf piece, that is, an article that is chipped or cracked that can be placed on display in such a manner so as not to reveal its damage. We suppose that there is some justification in doing this if the price and the piece warrant it. But there is little or no future in this kind of collecting, for there is no resale value. Collectors of experience rarely, if ever, deliberately buy a broken antique. In some instances, if the article is extremely rare and all the chips can be assembled, it is excusable. Furniture most often needs something replaced or repaired. But with glass, the damage is forever, and its value is most likely to be apparent only to its owner.

On the second day, one of the sheds was opened to reveal among other things several sleighs and a two-horse cutter of a kind rarely seen. The delicate ironwork of its runners was forged to attach the center pole in a rigid position. The horses on either side of the shaft would then be able to run free as the wind, pulling the cutter by the harness made for almost total freedom of their movement. This beautiful piece of the blacksmith's and carriage maker's art was rather like an early Currier and Ives print of the Hudson River Dutch.

Unfortunately, the soft goods and papers that appeared were in such a state that they were ready to be burned. Not so the collection of guns that appeared and was dated as early as the house itself. The guns were, in the main, of English manufacture, and although they were in excellent condition and brought high prices, the bids were lower than if their manufacture had been American. The crowd of the first day tired and lost interest, leaving the second day to the more dedicated antiquer. This was, of course, most usual, for a high proportion of onlookers at an auction is easily bored. Unless one is interested in buying, the novelty soon wears off, and if the viewer's knowledge of the articles is limited, his interest rapidly wanes.

This is not so with antiquers, for experience has proved, time and time again, that one of the most important attributes of putting together a successful collection is the quality of the collector's patience.

1860

Top across and bottom right: Four Sandwich glass plates, depicting an early sidewheel steamship, American eagle and stars with oak leaf, beehive, and acorn pattern and wreath. Boston and Sandwich Glass Company, 1835–1850.

Upper center: Painted tin tray depicting a steam locomotive and fuel car. Early Pennsylvania.

Bottom left and lower center: Two early weathervanes. Painted pine horse and rider inscribed with the date 1860, and angel weathervane carved of wood and polychromed in black, white, and gold. Hingham, Massachusetts, 1875–1890.

Top left: Blown-glass candlestick. Clear nonlead glass. Pennsylvania, eighteenth century.

Top center: Pennsylvania Dutch shrank. Walnut. This large wardrobe is of a type to be found in many Dutch homes. There were no closets built into the original stone structures. 1810–1820.

Top right: Blown-glass candlestick. Aquamarine-blue. 1850–1860.

Center: Two appliqué designs used on quilts. These typical motifs are a credit to the excellent primitive designing of the Pennsylvania Dutch housewife. The balance of color and form is beautiful. These patterns can be found in an infinite variety.

Bottom: Pennsylvania chest, child's size, 8" high, 18" across. A perfect example of decorated wood. Red, blue, green, black on a background of ivory white.

The word "scrim-
shaw" does not tell one
anything about the
history or romance of
this ancient art, which
is to decorate or carve
intricate designs on
whale, ivory, bone, or
even shells. Seamen
who sailed on ships all
over the world became
masters of this art form,
since their many
months at sea, often as
much as a year, gave
them the time, the
whalebone and walrus
teeth their materials,
and knives sharpened
to etching-tool points
their tools. It remained
for them only to
design the story that
they wished to portray
in this etched form.
Some, of course, were
more expert than
others, but whether the
results were more
professional or truly
primitive mattered very
little. The resulting
pieces are charming
objects of folk art and
are quite valuable
today. President
Kennedy's collection of
scrimshaw will no
doubt be exhibited to
the public in the near
future.

This art form is not exclusively American. Seamen all over the world have expressed their hopes and their loneliness in this art form.

The subject matter is, of course, predominantly of ships. Smaller carved objects such as whalebone pastry cutters were also made and presented as gifts to the sailor's loved one upon his arrival at home port.

Far right: A carved barometer. (Rhode Island School of Art)

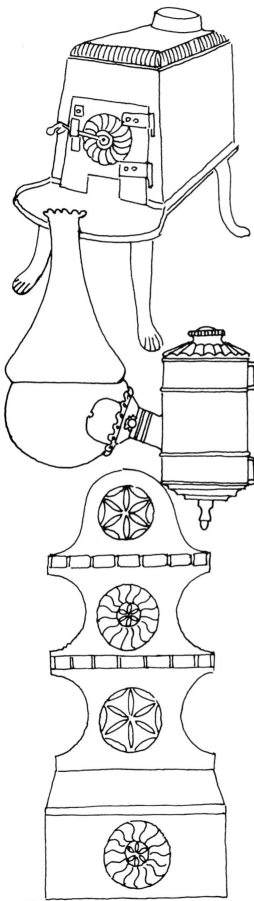

Top left: Primitive front-loading box-type heater. Large door in front to permit use of chunk wood. Has a base draft opening as part of its construction.

Center left: Nickel-plated Pullman lamp. Container holds a glass kerosene font with spring release. This wall-type lamp was used in many of the railroad cars prior to electricity.

Bottom left: Pennsylvania Dutch cutlery rack. Cut walnut with hex designs.

Top right: Wrought-iron whirling broiler with serpentine forgings. These very practical broilers permitted the cook to rotate the broiler over the flames. Probably the first of the "lazy Susans."

Center right: Small corner cupboard with painted decoration. (Metropolitan Museum)

Bottom right: Majolica pitcher, raised sunflower design on both sides. Pewter top. Made in Pennsylvania. American Majolica was also made in Baltimore, Trenton, Ohio, New York, and New Hampshire from 1880 to 1892. (Authors' collection)

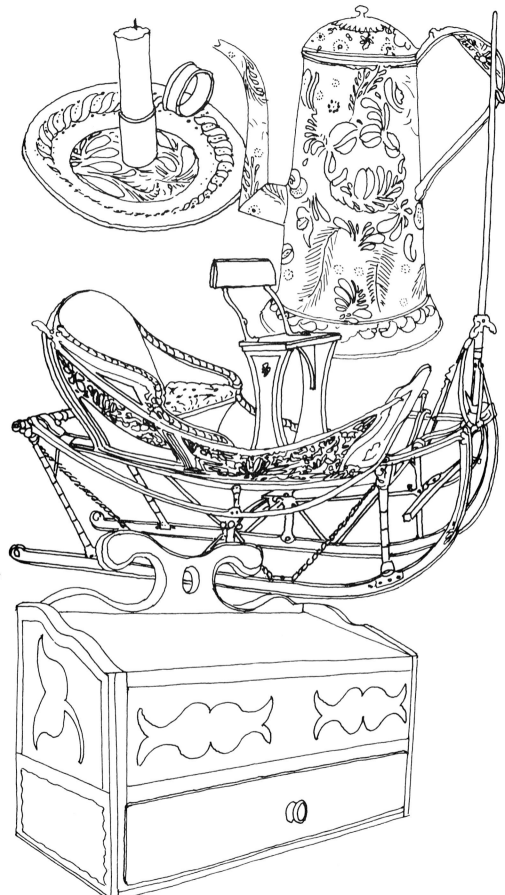

Top: Pennsylvania tinware. This candlestick and the accompanying coffee pot are an example of the fine tinsmith work done throughout Pennsylvania. The decorations are typical and traditional.

Center: The two-horse cutter shown here is an example of fine carriage work done all along the Hudson Valley. Authors' collection includes a cutter much like the one illustrated and it was purchased in New York State.

Bottom: Salt was important and in short supply. It was kept dry in this kind of box kept near the stove. 1800s. In some instances, these wall boxes were used to store tobacco, but it was also in short supply and usually preserved in smaller quantities.

Top left: Brass-based table lamp with opaque shade. Kerosene. This type of lamp was very popular and was distributed widely. It came in a variety of metal design bases.

Top right: Coffee mill. Pewter coffee font, pine box and drawer. Mills of this type were made in quantity for home use as early as 1840.

Right margin: Excellent example of forging. A sawtooth trammel. Berks County, Pennsylvania. Trammels of this type made the raising or lowering of pots cooking over the fire a simple effort.

Center: Punched tin coffee pot, brass top with hardwood finial. Traditional Dutch motif.

Bottom: Cherry butterfly table is unusual because it is also a trestle table and has a drawer at either end. Lancaster County, Pennsylvania.

40

Top left: Free-blown flask, dark-green lead-free glass. Two-piece mold with eagle design. 1830–1850.

Center left: Common brass lamp with blown chimney. These simple carrying lamps were made in massive amounts and sold almost everywhere. 1850.

Top right: Bobbin wheel was used to prepare the yarn for the loom. The thread was finished by additional twisting and stretching. (Authors' collection)

Center: Small Queen Anne sofa with shell carving on legs, drake feet, gracefully scrolled back, and comfortable rolled arms. Middle eighteenth century. (Metropolitan Museum)

Bottom center: Complex tin chandelier. Tin arms are welded to the body with a pewter-type compound. This chandelier carries sixteen candles. Made in New England, early nineteenth century.

Bottom right: Pressed-glass water glass. Late Victorian.

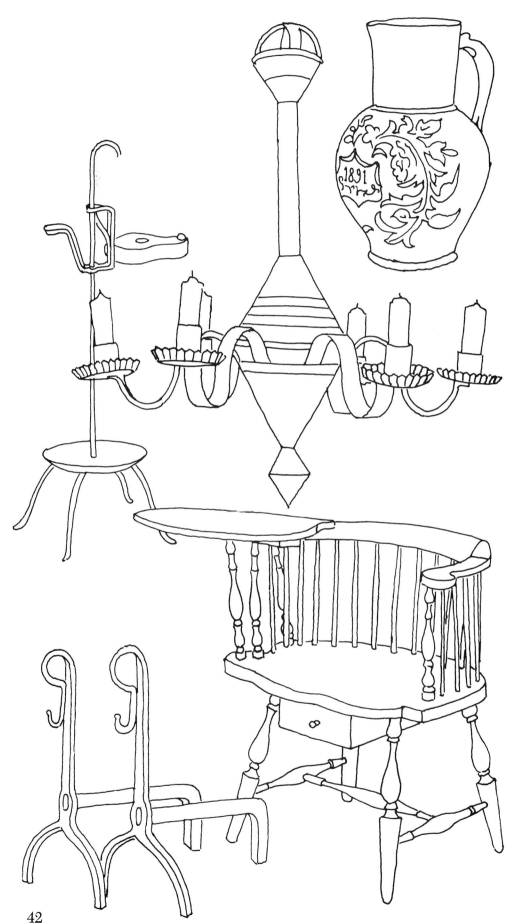

Top left: Betty lamp on wrought-iron stand with vertical adjustment. Solid base.

Bottom left: Wrought-iron andirons with looped finials, rack for fire fork and split hooks.

Top center: Early six-candle, heavy tin candelabrum. Hard-wood center turning, probably maple or oak for weight. New England and Pennsylvania. Early eighteenth century.

Top right: Salt glaze earthenware pitcher, 1891. An example of contemporary "artware." This artware became very popular, and although some of the ultimate designs left something to be desired, time has interested the collectors and these are now an interesting part of Americana.

Bottom right: Pennsylvania Windsor armchair with writing platform. Drawer under seat for writing materials. 1770–1780.

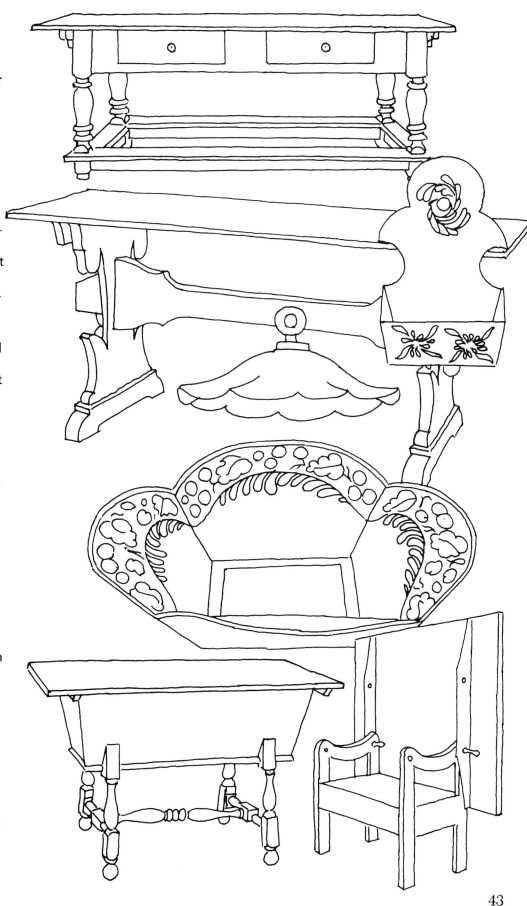

Top: Pennsylvania Dutch table with removable breadboard top and two deep drawers. This particular table is of beechwood and painted a barn red. Can be found made of walnut or oak and unpainted.

Upper left: Pennsylvania trestle table, walnut. The unusual keys to hold the center-board are mortised through the narrow part of the legs. The top is a removable breadboard. 1810.

Upper right: Decorated matchholder. Freehand painted on tin. Were also constructed of cast iron or brass.

Upper center: Milk-glass smoke bell. These very practical hangings are to protect the ceilings from lampwick smoke. Are found in brass, tin, and pewter.

Lower center: Decorated tin bread tray. Pennsylvania, 1750. Most of these pieces were painted freehand, and without decals.

Bottom left: Pine dough tray, referred to as a "dough trough." Pennsylvania, eighteenth century.

Bottom right: Bench table. Hutch table construction. Wooden pins serve as hinges. Often used for a fireplace seat, to permit the high reflective surface of the back to supplement the fire's heat.

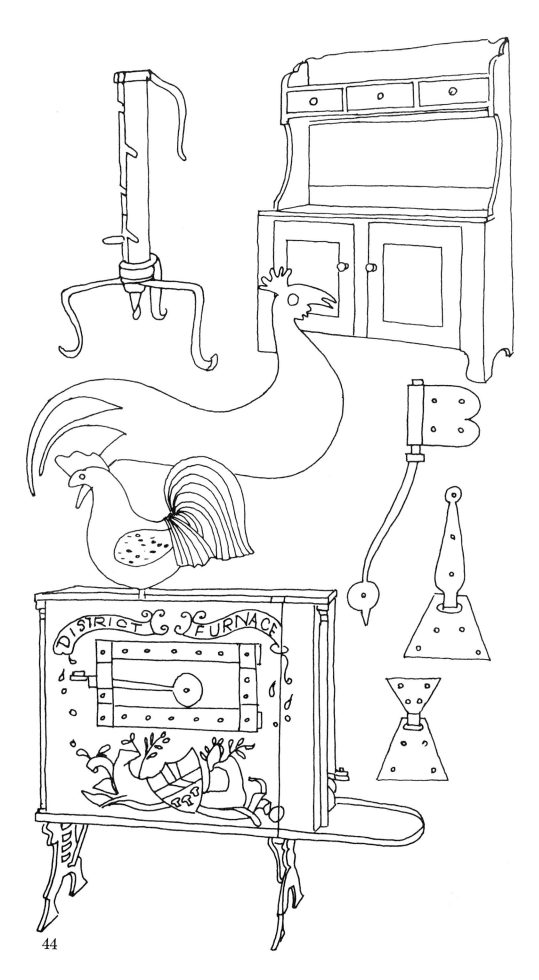

Top left: Early sheet-iron candlestick. Notched in order to change height of candle. (Landis Valley Museum)

Center and bottom left: Two decorated weathervanes. Rooster of wood bas-relief and painted. Graceful rooster made of sheet metal. Pennsylvania, 1800. Cast-iron stove with maker's name in relief. Berks County, Pennsylvania, 1820.

Top right: Water bench with scrolled sides and top. Three drawers. Pine. Berks County, Pennsylvania, 1840.

Center and lower right: Three types of wrought-iron hinges. Rat-tail type is extremely primitive forging; door can be lifted without removal of hinge. Two linked hinges are butterfly and wedge and strap. With iron in short supply in New England, all metal work was of fine quality. Forgings with little waste was the order of the times.

44

The Painted
Barn Auction
in Eastern
Pennsylvania

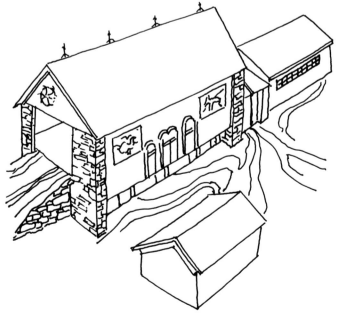

The word "auction," according to the dictionary, comes from the Latin word *auctio*, an increasing, from *augere*, to increase. The first definition is a public sale of property to the highest bidder, usually by a person authorized and licensed for that purpose. Now we do not know if auctions have been going on since Roman times or even before. But travel has convinced us that the more ancient the society or country we visit, the more we are expected to haggle over the purchase price of an article that has caught our fancy.

We are led to believe that auctions have been going on since the beginning of recorded history. The emotions involving the participants are probably as primitive and essential to most people as gambling.

Years before radio, television, or the movies, there was a time-honored Yankee custom called "horse trading." Haggling over a price was an accepted practice in the old country, and it certainly found its way across the Atlantic in the very earliest of colonial times.

The South had its slave market. Later came its cotton and sugar markets. The North's tea exchange conducted for the profit of English royalty would have made a rug merchant of any nationality envious. All these ancient business habits, or motivations, were practiced and accepted here and must have satisfied the skills and pleasures of those participating.

A bargain, in today's accepted sense of the word, is something that is bought for less than its known value, and the possibility of that happy end result is what keeps auctions thriving.

In the rural sections of Pennsylvania, entertainment was and still is in short supply, particularly the kind of entertainment that an entire family can enjoy. A place where people can congregate and talk and eat and experience something of suspense. A place with no admission charge and none of the formidable exertion of dancing. The public auction sale in the evening became the perfect answer. When chores were done, people would get together, sell something they didn't want, buy something they didn't need, and take their families out for an evening's entertainment at no cost to themselves other than their own impulse buying. To bid higher than their peers gave them the bonus of an "ego trip," whether or not their bid was the final one.

The whole activity probably started with the cattle and horse auctions, then came the produce market and auction, and now there are literally hundreds of night sales. They are not forced sales in the legal sense, as is an estate sale to satisfy creditors. Their purpose is to fill community centers with people and merchandise and sell the latter to the former. Merchandise that is new, second- or third-hand, intact, broken, or patched, is carried to these auction barns by the wagonload. Everything and anything imaginable that may be salable emerges at these sales. All sales are final and "as is," which means if it's broken or won't work, the bidder must find that out before bidding. The auction house wants a commission on the turnover, plus the profit on the sale of the food concessions. And in Pennsylvania that food profit is considerable.

These unique events go on almost every Wednesday or Saturday night, while others take place on Saturday afternoons. They can be found in or near almost every good-sized town in Pennsylvania. The Painted Barn is just one of them. An attempt to describe the variety of merchandise that is offered at the Painted Barn auctions on Wednesday evenings would be impossible. To see it is to believe it, and one only has to be there promptly at eight.

The Painted Barn is located in one of the most beautiful areas of all of eastern Pennsylvania, a little-traveled district in the vicinity of Virginsville and Windsor Castle. That entire valley contains large, well-kept farms with huge dairy barns, many of which are beautifully decorated with primitive murals. The quaint and attractive idea of barn paintings is typical of the Pennsylvania Dutch farm. The decorating has a long history, dating far back into early colonial times.

Itinerant artists, such as the well-known Rufus Porter, were exponents of this unusual American folk art. Porter, a most versatile man, applied his creative talents in many areas. A farm boy from Boxford, Massachusetts, he set out to paint and decorate whatever surface excited his interest. Portraits, barns, interiors of houses, his compulsive need to decorate seemed insatiable. His expansive talent and energy led him into teaching, music, and professional dancing. It is said that his unique inventiveness was of a variety that would lead to his being called a Yankee Leonardo da Vinci. As founder and editor of the now defunct *New York Magazine* and the present day *Scientific American*, he wrote one of the first books on landscape painting. It was published in 1825, when Porter was in his early thirties, and his book, *The Curious Arts*, enjoyed a rather wide circulation.

Porter was reputed to have decorated over 150 homes throughout New England. He was not, however, alone in this talent and capability. A Joseph Leavitt was blazing an artistic trail through the same New England countryside at about the same time.

This decorating of barns was an idea particularly favored in Pennsylvania, for the Dutch people of that countryside had little or no resistance to color. Given a bucket of paint of almost any color, the rural Pennsylvania farmer could not wait to apply it somewhere—almost anywhere. What with hex signs and simulated doors painted on the solid walls of their barns, there was no stopping them. Murals of cows, horses, chickens, flags, eagles—almost any kind of subject matter—were painted for all the countryside to see. The Painted Barn was just one of many of those interesting examples.

When we have attended this kind of auction, there have always been several very fine pieces of early Dutch furnishings displayed. They are, however, rarely put up for sale, and contrary to the performance of the estate sale, if they are put up they are withdrawn if the bids do not reach the seller's desired price. These antiques are used, as we know it in modern merchandising, as window dressing or as "loss leaders," that is, without the loss of the item on view. It is rarely, if ever, sold. This is not to say that there are not many fine bargains to be had at these sales. For with the enormous tonnage of things that is brought in, there are bound to be many opportunities for antiquers. All one has to do is have great patience and time to wade through the sale of toasters, washing machines, obsolete vacuum cleaners, and radios that are not quite early enough to interest a collector or even a dealer in antique appliances.

For one who might be just starting to furnish a country place, however, the pickings are unexcelled. Garden equipment, shovels, rakes, hoes, hand-tillers, seeds of dubious quality, and flower pots of all sizes and materials are usually brought out for sale. Canning jars—some old, some new, some chipped, some blue—exist by the case. The bids on these, naturally, fluctuate by the season. During the fall or late summer when farm produce is abundant, preserving objects are eagerly sought and bid for accordingly. By and large, the furniture is of the worst kind, often coming from local furniture outlets attempting to convert some of their least attractive pieces into cash. But even the worst-looking couch, if well built, can be slipcovered with a simple material to camouflage the homely fabric or the tasteless carvings of the frame. One thing that can be counted on is the fact that if it were made to be marketed in the Pennsylvania countryside, it would have to have been built "for strong," as the Dutch saying goes.

Dishes are usually in sets and of poor quality, but a bidder always should be on the alert for a piece of ironstone china or blue willowware that is not Japanese. We have seen dishes of flow-blue that somehow or other found themselves on display, and occasionally a bit of Majolica, carnival glass, and even a piece of salt-glaze. These, basically, are not antiques auctions, yet fine pieces do slip in unnoticed. Pressed glass of all patterns is occasionally mixed in with a fine piece of cut glass. Jugs and pickling jars are also likely to turn up. It is rather disconcerting to see a good collection of ironstone sold in separate pieces; heaven knows how long it took the seller to get it all together. But as I cautioned before, patience and buying the pieces one at a time with a variety of bids may average out at a bargain price.

For those who have been putting sets together for a long time, this is a great place for pairing odd pieces or finding parts. At a time when a wick for a kerosene lamp is hard to buy, we have seen boxes of them in all widths put up for bid.

Relish or jam preserves are chancy, but if you are fearless, bid. At the very least, the jelly glasses and canning jars are reusable. Pennsylvania farm wives are well known for some types of canning, and we have bought and eaten relishes for which we wish we had recipes. Not too long ago, sausage, smoked hams, and bacons were regular items at these sales. We miss the fried smoked pork chops cut from the loin that were a special hefty delicacy of the countryside.

Paint is a popular item here, but likely to be of second-rate quality. When it comes to tools, the older ones, if in one piece, are more likely to be of better quality than the newer ones, which surprisingly seem to fetch a higher price at auction than if one were to buy them at a retail store. I guess everyone gets caught up in the bidding, and the actual value of an item becomes unimportant.

The popularity of an auction rarely has to do with the quality of merchandise that is sold. All things considered, the proliferation of "stuff" is much the same at all of these sales. The local people go where their friends can be found and where they like the auctioneer. If the first auction that you attend is not interesting or enjoyable, try another place, for the atmosphere is always local.

Local papers carry advertisements for auctions in their "For Sale" columns. The ads can be recognized by their lack of legal notifications, and they are repeated week after week.

As a matter of preference, however, we rarely attend an auction that is not an estate sale. The reasons are quite simple. We prefer that all sales be final and go to the highest bidder. Also, we like the opportunity of inspecting the articles that will be auctioned at least an hour or two prior to bidding. It is very important to us that everything at the sale be put up for bidding, for we find it entirely unsatisfactory to see an exhibit of desirable pieces that are for display only. If our motive were to look, we would be more likely to go to a museum. In all fairness, however, country auction sales are interesting experiences and as much a part of the American rural scene as small county fairs.

Top left: Eight-day clock made by F. N. Welch Company, 1880. This late Victorian clock was manufactured by many clockmakers and sold in the thousands.

Bottom left: Fireman's hat. Made of leather and decorated with red lacquer and gold leaf, it shed water from back of neck and protected the face from the heat of fire.

Top right: Fire chief's trumpet. Late Victorian. Actually this was used as a megaphone, not as a true horn. Often a presentation piece.

Bottom right: Barber-shop sign made of wood and painted with red and white striping.

Top left: Delicate cast-iron wall bracket kerosene lamp with mercury glass reflector. Thumbprint cranberry glass shade and brass burner fittings.

Bottom left: Pressed glass kerosene table lamp. This pedestal is hand-painted. Often a clear glass pedestal was filled with dried flowers. Metal work is of polished brass castings. 1850.

Top right: Silver toddy strainer by Paul Revere. The long handles are designed to allow it to rest on the rim of either tankard or punch bowl.

Center right: Milk glass smoke bell.

Bottom right: Classic Queen Anne walnut tavern table. The brass drawer pulls are of fine design and polished brass. Very early eighteenth century.

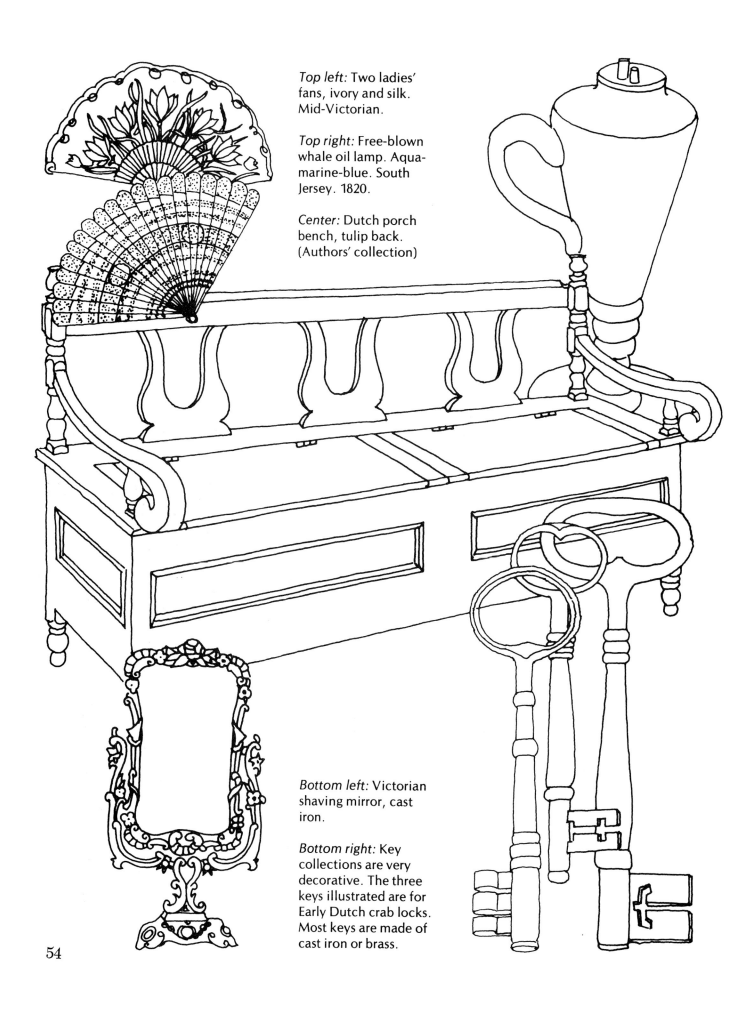

Top left: Two ladies' fans, ivory and silk. Mid-Victorian.

Top right: Free-blown whale oil lamp. Aquamarine-blue. South Jersey. 1820.

Center: Dutch porch bench, tulip back. (Authors' collection)

Bottom left: Victorian shaving mirror, cast iron.

Bottom right: Key collections are very decorative. The three keys illustrated are for Early Dutch crab locks. Most keys are made of cast iron or brass.

54

Top left: Three wine-glasses of clear lead glass, blown and decorated with star cutting and copper-wheel engraving. Early eighteenth century.

Bottom left: Platform rocker by Charles Eastlake. These designs were based on early Jacobean forms, sometimes referred to as Neo-Gothic, and the "homelike style." Late Victorian.

Top right: Porcelain and bronze kerosene lamp. Hand-painted globe. Japanese influence, late Victorian.

Center right: Iron casting of top section of hitching post. Early eighteenth century.

Bottom right: An inlaid table, carved and gilt ornamentation. Made in New York about 1865. Reflects the Italian influence.

Top left: Decorative bird carved of wood and brightly painted. Berks County, Pennsylvania.

Center left: Toleware bread tray from Lebanon, Pennsylvania. Decal and hand-painting on heavy tin.

Bottom left: Dutch cooking crane with unusual forgings, curled brace. Berks County, Pennsylvania, 1800. Forged "S" hook. These pothooks to hang over cranes were of different lengths in order to regulate the pot's height from the fire.

Top right: Pennsylvania corner cupboards are most effective when placed one over the other. The brass hinges are a reproduction of early rat-tail hinges. 1820–1840.

Bottom right: Punched tin coffee pot with vase and flower design and brass knob on top lid. Unpainted. Pennsylvania, 1820.

56

Top left: Ornamental flatiron stand. These decorative cast-iron castings are in innumerable designs and were cast until the end of the nineteenth century. Later they were constructed of sheet iron.

Upper left center: Ironstone china tureen, one of a great many patterns all made in quantity.

Lower left center: Early two-wick pewter lamp. Meant originally to burn whale oil, but could burn fats and later low-grade petroleum fuel.

Bottom left: Mahogany tilting top candlestand on "birdcage." Eighteenth century.

Top right: Wrought-iron boot scraper. Forged. 1800s.

Center right: Punched tin lantern, which predates glass lantern. Made in great quantity both in New England and Pennsylvania. Early eighteenth century.

Bottom right: Kerosene lamp with nickel plate over brass font and base. Simple opaque glass shade. 1897.

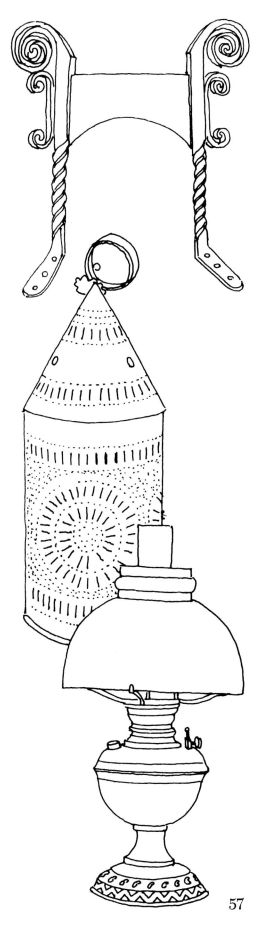

57

Top left: Celery glass or vase blown of clear lead glass. Elaborate copper-wheel engraving on upper part of body. Early nineteenth century.

Center and top right: Blown three-mold footed bowl of clear lead glass. Blown three-mold foot is also of clear lead glass and is applied to bowl. Sunburst motif is on both pieces. Probably made by Boston and Sandwich Glass Company, early 1800s. Vase or celery glass on top right is probably the same manufacturer and period.

Bottom left and right: Four pieces of shell-and-jewel-pattern pressed glass. Maker unknown, mid-Victorian. (Authors' collection)

58

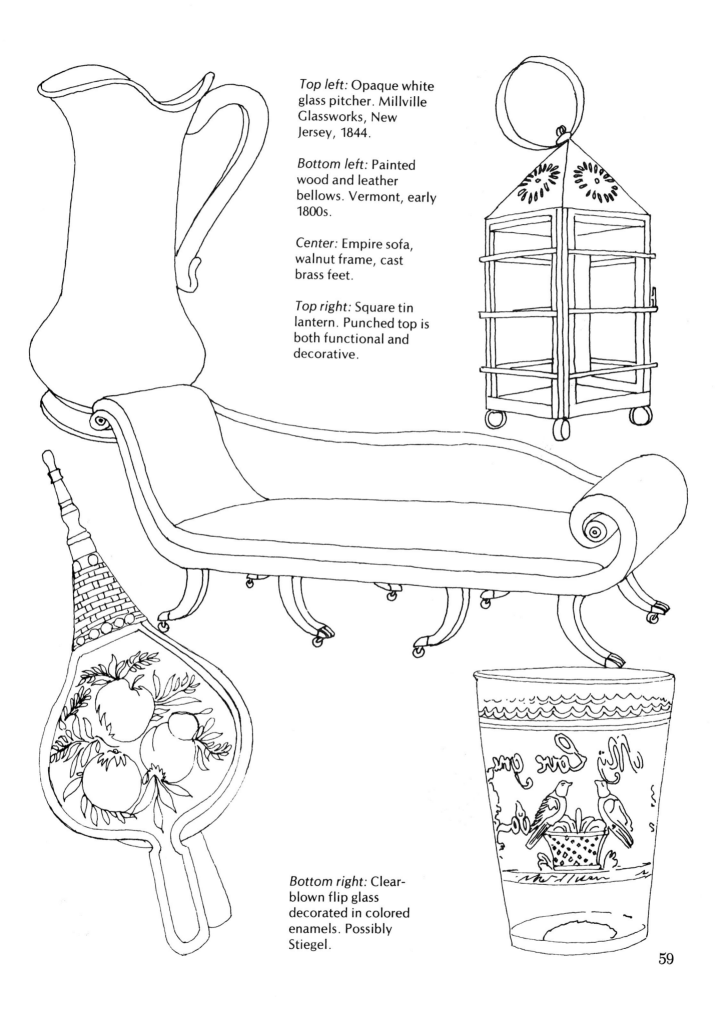

Top left: Opaque white glass pitcher. Millville Glassworks, New Jersey, 1844.

Bottom left: Painted wood and leather bellows. Vermont, early 1800s.

Center: Empire sofa, walnut frame, cast brass feet.

Top right: Square tin lantern. Punched top is both functional and decorative.

Bottom right: Clear-blown flip glass decorated in colored enamels. Possibly Stiegel.

59

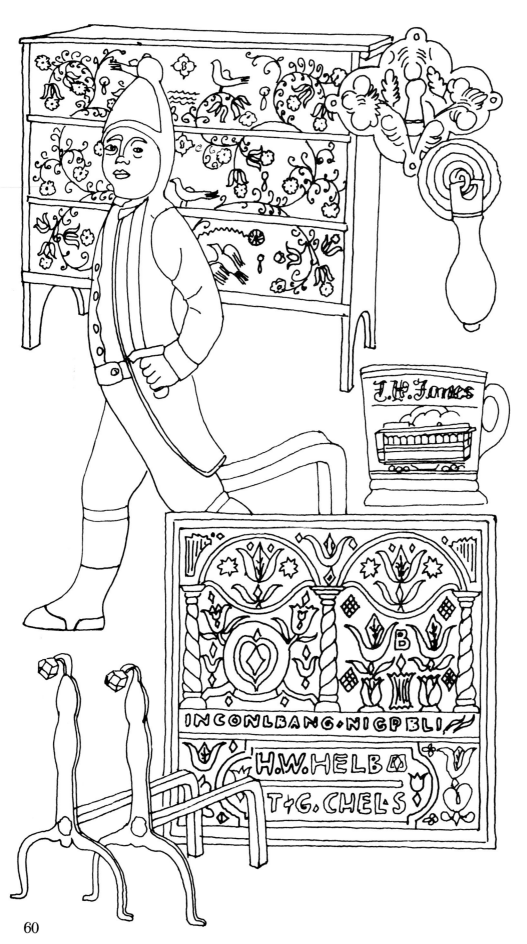

Top left: Painted pine blanket chest. Top opens to a deep top well for storage. The mock drawers are the two top ones. This appears to be Pennsylvania Dutch but was found in Massachusetts.

Center left: Cast-iron Hessian soldier andiron. These interesting castings were made late in the eighteenth century.

Bottom left: Rare gooseneck andirons. These wrought-iron pieces were often mistaken for the rattlesnake design.

Top right: Stamped brass escutcheon and drawer pull.

Center right: Shaving mugs were in popular demand as early as 1860. Generally they were imported from Bavaria without decoration and were decorated in barber shops to the specifications of each customer, often carrying a symbol of his daily occupation.

Bottom right: Stove plate or fireback. These heavy castings were the back reflectors of heat in an open fireplace and made to order to each owner's specifications. They were the first step from a fireplace to a stove.

60

Top left: Country wash-stand found in Waterloo, New York, was decorated freehand rather than the usual stencil. This charming bedroom furnishing predates indoor plumbing and was replaced, most unfortunately, by a wash sink in most country bedrooms. The china bowl and pitcher set were often beautifully decorated glazed pottery.

Bottom left: Pewter flagon. The handle, lid, and thumbpiece are of English design and the body of the flagon indicates Teutonic influences. Lancaster County, Pennsylvania, late eighteenth century.

Top right and bottom right: Three redware plates. Sgraffito and slipware. Primitive colors limited to white, black, and green on red-brown background.

Center right: A pewter teapot with hardwood handle. Pennsylvania, eighteenth century.

61

Top left: Stoneware crock with cobalt-blue slip decoration on usual slate-gray glaze. These blue designs included birds, animals, and conventional brush-stroke design. 1850–1870.

Center left: Stamped-brass keyhole escutcheon and matching teardrop handle. Early eighteenth century.

Bottom left: Two-burner kerosene angle lamp, sometimes referred to as a Pullman lamp. Nickel over brass fonts, upper chimney opaque white with clear glass bases. (*Authors' collection*)

Top right: Two brass escutcheons of rather common design. Lower one attributed to Chippendale. Keyhole was not always complemented with lock.

Center: Polychromed bottle with conventional birds and flowers of Pennsylvania Dutch design. (Philadelphia Museum of Art)

Bottom right: This simple water bench was typical of primitive kitchens. Buckets of water were placed on lower shelf and wash basins were on upper shelf.

Auction at the Chicken Farm in Lehigh Valley

The Chicken Farm was nestled on the northern slope of a hill facing a small treeless valley. If one were to tunnel through the hill that the farm rested on, the opening on the far end would face directly onto the center of the Lehigh Valley. Maiden Creek flowed slowly past farms to the south and east. The Pennsylvania Dutch, who settled in the hills bordering the Lehigh Valley on both the north and the south, did not do this by choice. As excellent and knowledgeable farmers, they knew the value of the deep bottomland of the valley. But others got there first, and some had the means to secure the better and more productive land. The Pennsylvania Dutch settled where and for what they could.

The location of the Chicken Farm was in one of the poorer places. The owners probably produced what they could on the shale of their farm's slopes: goats, chickens, and sheep, as well as their one product for market, eggs. It was not an expansive life, but they had the comfort of a solid house and the security of being able to produce food and salable items sufficient for their needs.

The narrow valley facing the house was fed by a good spring, and with care and work its overflow could be used to irrigate the grass around it sufficiently to feed one or two head of cattle. This never became a reality, however, for the owners had to spend too many of their man-hours working for other farmers to pay for the feed for the chickens. And taxes were paid for by work on the county roads, so there was no time for irrigation projects.

The house was small, and its thick walls served to protect against the winter cold and the steamy heat of the Pennsylvania summer. Their children were gone now; the hard and repetitive existence on the farm was not for them. They wanted to see the world, even if the desire got them only as far as Allentown or Reading. The house, built of fieldstone and mortared with clay and horsehair, was typical of the poorer homes of the early 1800s. Originally, the roofs were made of slate, a commodity that was readily available in that area. But as the shingles got old and brittle, they were covered over with corrugated iron or tar paper in order to stay the major leaks.

The Pennsylvania Dutch people who settled in and around Moselem Springs were more frugal than their valley neighbors. Their low-country, German background of hard living led them to expect little in the way of luxury. However, they had learned to take care of what they had. It was practically impossible for one of this background to throw anything away, for ingenuity in reusing and making do was a fact of life. Unfortunately, the necessity of earning took precedence over saving. It was academic that time would ultimately win, and unhappily the house, barn, property, and contents would be sold for taxes.

The poor look of the Chicken Farm and its outbuildings is no criteria for judging the objects that may emerge. Certainly, anyone with a little experience cannot expect great quantities of antiques to appear. The ceilings are not high enough for a Queen Anne chest-on-chest or a canopy bed. But there are boxes upon boxes of hundred-year-old junk in the sheds. And don't forget that a lot of collectors have gotten mighty rich on someone else's junk.

Advertisements of the sale appeared in most of the local papers, with lengthy lists of items to be sold. But to the experienced, it was apparent that a house that poor could never have held the pieces listed. It is not unusual for some sales to display antiques that never were a part of that particular property. This is not dishonest nor indicative of a desire of the auctioneer to fool anyone. There is simply an antique someone wants to sell, and an auction constitutes a reasonable marketplace. It really is an added opportunity for the buyer.

Those who are experienced in attending auctions and are capable of estimating the kind and quality of the antiques sold from each house, really do not care what is put up for sale. They either know long in advance what is there and what they are willing to bid for, or they bid for things that strike their fancy as impetuously as the totally un-initiated. Experts often make more mistakes than the unknowing and, I might add, have a lot less fun. A dealer or expert is at the extreme disadvantage of being recognized, particularly if he is seen to bid on an object. This is likely to up the bids from those who are not so much in-terested in an antique as in the fact that the expert wants it. These be-hind-the-scenes activities at auctions cause experts to appoint others to bid for them. Often a group will appoint one of the least known of their group to do all the bidding for the day. They simply specify the things they want and the price that they are willing to pay.

All this, it would seem, puts the individual collector at an enormous disadvantage. Nothing could be further from the truth. The dealer is probably at the auction to buy an antique for resale. He must buy it for a price that will allow him to sell it for a profit. A private collector is not restricted in this way, and if he bids a little more than the dealer bids, he makes his purchase for what might be called a bit over the dealer cost. Another disadvantage for a dealer is that he may be on assignment to buy for a collector who cannot attend. This, of course, puts the antique right up in open auction, and your bid is simply against another collector's bid. A dealer may also be bidding for his private collection (and I never met a dealer who didn't have one). If what he is bidding for is worth that much to him as an expert, it may be worth that much to you, if you can afford it.

It is sometimes quite amusing to watch the antics of a dealer or a collector trying to disguise his bids. What with winks, the slightest of head nods, mouth twitchings, hat brim pullings, faint whistles, and the movement of one finger, it is all a great wonder the auctioneer can catch his bid at all. But auctioneers have an eye for a bid, and experience teaches them to spot these subtle movements, for it is most important for them to have a following of buyers. A good auctioneer is only as good as the total gross of his sales. He must entertain the crowd, not bore them; he must never drag bids out to the very last penny. An auctioneer must exude good humor and patience, for nothing turns a crowd off as fast and permanently as a grouchy or threatening attitude on his part.

At most auctions the man who finally buys everything that no one wants to bid on is the junk dealer. His bid used to be an automatic one—a nickel. He is still there at every auction and his bid is still open for the unwanted articles, but inflation has doubled his bid to a dime, although he is, and probably always will be, referred to as the "nickel man." I have often watched his ultimate and automatic purchases and thought of what fun it must be for him to discover just one thing worth twenty cents in each ten-cent purchase he has brought home from an auction. One hundred percent profit and a day's fun, too.

At an auction near Lyon Valley, Pennsylvania, held usually every second or third year, a nickel man resells the articles he has bought over the years. Some he has repaired, others he has simply cleaned and polished; he has paired articles to increase their value, and boxed the jars he found, one at a time, into dozens. He has combined zinc lids with blue Ball jars, put parts of lamps into labeled boxes, repaired chairs with rungs of other chairs, and joined short links of chain into usable lengths. Clockworks and small parts are boxed and labeled, and wheels are paired according to size. The papers and rags and reusable metals have, of course, already been sold, and the gross taken in that day makes one much more careful not to return from any auction empty-handed.

Food at an auction doesn't have to be good. But there should be and usually is lots of it. For if nothing else happens at an auction, you do get an appetite; maybe it's the fresh air and the excitement. Usually, ladies from a local church will cater an auction and provide you with large barbequed sandwiches, chock-full of relish and raw onion, shoofly pies, and Cokes and coffee.

When the furnishings start to come out and are placed in the front yard, the quantity of stuff even a small house holds never ceases to be amazing. The dunker chest with its crude iron hinges and heavy hand-planed surface is one of the articles you would expect to find in a primitive house of this kind. There would have to be at least twenty kerosene lamps, the hanging type, or bracket lamps, as well as table lamps. Remember, this house was built years before Thomas Edison was born. The half-spindle chairs have lost most of their original decals, and some have been painted over a bright blue. Nevertheless, the plank seats are intact, and with a bit of elbow grease and paint remover they will make a fine set of primitive chairs. Never mind if one has a hole cut out of the seat; one is found in practically every family of chairs.

The jelly cupboard is probably made of beechwood or tulip, and if finished in a grayed barn red, it will add to any room in your house—dining room, den, or bedroom. A butcher bench or two is bound to be in the cellar, and there are probably a couple more in the shed near the chicken houses. Jugs and crocks will exist by the dozen—remember that people in this area pickled and preserved as much as they had crocks and jars to hold. The clock from the kitchen wall will not in all probability be the mantel type, but a schoolhouse Ingraham has become a rarity today. If there is a clock on the mantel, it might just be a brass one commemorating Teddy Roosevelt and his charge up San Juan Hill, or the sinking of the *Maine*. In either case, it is a collector's item, particularly if a big brass eagle hovers over the scene of flags, swords, and sinkings.

You may not have room for a farm wagon in your suburban home, but in that pile of old harnesses are the bits of brightwork that decorated the horses' blinders or brass buckles and whiffletrees with hand-forged ironwork. They make the most attractive of primitive chandeliers for a bar or rec room. Don't forget old wheels, even if the spokes are broken—the iron tire can be welded into the most useful firewood holder that ever graced a terrace.

A farm that has no tractor usually has wheelbarrows. An early one of wood with a wood wheel is a museum piece. Even a metal one with an inflated or deflated tire may save you a lot of lugging some day. Early primitive tools are not only valuable, but wonderful to decorate with.

There is every reason to believe that there must be a box of old molding planes or a wooden block and fall in a house as old as this.

The cast-iron apple-butter pot probably still has its original trivet, and, if one is not careful, he may miss the bid on those old oak barrels. You may never make wine, but if you do, there's nothing like an old barrel.

You can be sure that the things you buy you will see again somewhere else for higher prices. It's all part of the treasure hunt and the day in the country. Enjoy it, for the day of the country auction will not go on forever. Once these small and ancient houses expose and dispose of their valuables, they cannot do it a second time.

Top left: Punched-tin pie safe used for ventilated storage cabinet. Berks County, Pennsylvania, 1800. The holes in the top of each stanchion allowed the piece to hang from the ceiling in order to provide safety from vermin in the cool of the cellar.

Bottom left and top right: Wrought-iron cooking utensils. Most all of this period were forged to order, and handle length as well as size were tailored to each housewife's specifications.

Center: Dough tray used for breadmaking. Box is for rising dough, and top, when inverted, becomes a kneading board. These dough trays were made in a variety of shapes, heights, and capacities. Each was tailored to the individual housewife's needs.

Bottom right: Pennsylvania dry sink with breadboard top. Pine. The dovetail detail on sink basin is especially good workmanship, as are the slant sides. Nineteenth century. Dry sinks held the dishpan for washing eating and cooking utensils. The used water was carried out. The sink provided nothing except a table for the daily chore.

Top left: Very primitive spider fireplace pan; long legs, which set into fireplace ash, and long handle are integral parts of this important cooking utensil.

Top right and center left: Painted tin coffee pot. Lebanon, Pennsylvania. To its left, a painted cookie box with familiar "distelfink" motif. The hasp is typical of latches on Pennsylvania tinware.

Center: High bench seat with drawer. Beechwood. Berks County, Pennsylvania, 1825. Many of these primitive household pieces were homemade or a product of the local carpenter. What they usually had in common was durability. Many, of course, were of very primitive design, making them all the more sought-after.

Center right: Early three-legged milking stool. Lancaster, Pennsylvania.

Bottom right: Very early Pennsylvania pinewood box. The primitive decoration resembles the scrollwork found on early slipware or redware.

71

Top left: Early Pennsylvania sawbuck table with removable top, unusual foot rests, and scrolled sawbuck legs. 1750. (Philadelphia Museum of Art)

Bottom left: Pennsylvania walnut corner cupboard with turned wood finials and brass "H" hinges. Eighteenth century. A cupboard with solid wood doors is often referred to as a "blind" cupboard.

Top right: Primitive cross base candle stand. Maple and pine. 1780. A great many of these lovely pieces were so delicately constructed that time has taken its toll. Originally intended to support a light, this was about all the weight they could take.

Bottom right: Mid-nineteenth-century balloon-back chair with plank seat of poplar. Shaped and designed for comfort. The round back and spindles are made of maple or hickory. A basic color of green or brown, they were decorated with stencils of popular motifs.

72

Top left: Early Pennsylvania cutlery rack made of beechwood and deep cut with traditional Dutch designs.

Far left: Pine-type trammel, quite as practical as the sawtooth type but forging is more primitive. Pennsylvania, 1800. Decorative crane hook.

Center left: S-shaped hook used for shortening chains. Pennsylvania, 1800.

Near left: Early skimmer and ladle, typical heavy Pennsylvania forgings.

Top right: Decorated and turned wood egg cup. Pennsylvania. Eighteenth century.

Upper right center: Primitive butter scoop. Pine. These were found all through the Northeast. Earliest said to be from New England.

Lower right center: Double sawtooth trammel with fine forgings, made to hang from fireplace crane. Pennsylvania, 1800. Typical Teutonic influence on the forging.

Bottom right: Pennsylvania noodle board made of chestnut, 26" long, 1" thick. Later "boards" were made of slate, mined and made in Berks County, Pennsylvania.

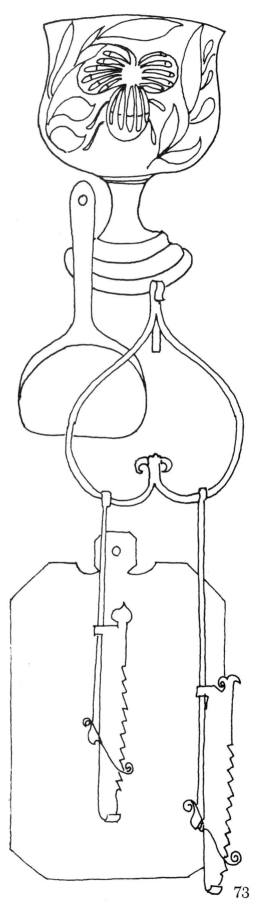

73

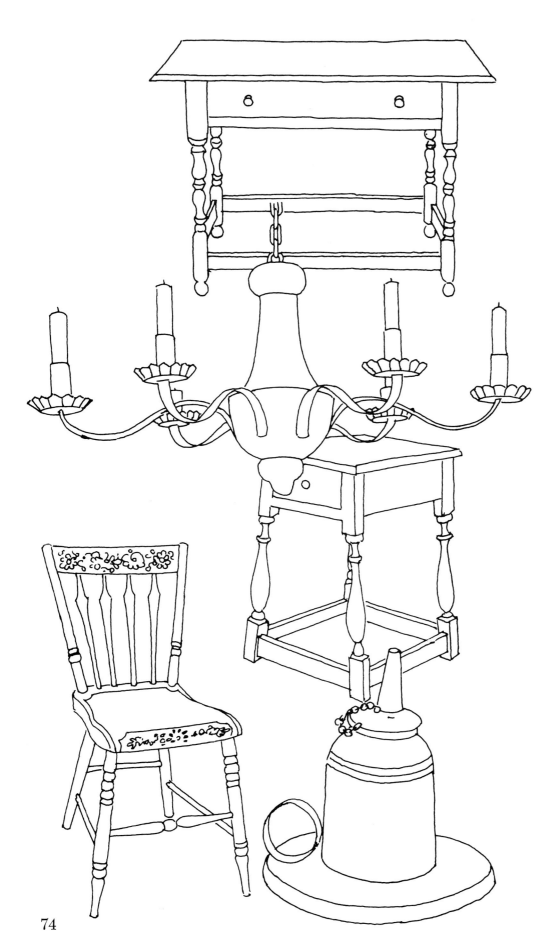

Top right: Maple-and-pine tavern table. Single large drawer with maple peg pulls is characteristic of early eighteenth-century construction in this area. The stretcher base added much to the strength and support of the table.

Center: This late eighteenth-century tin chandelier has a wood body under the tin covering. The six tin branches are a noteworthy economy, for some of the tin chandeliers are made to hold twelve and fifteen candles for the more extravagant user.

Center right: Splay-leg table made of maple with one-board pine top. Middle eighteenth century.

Bottom right: Tin whale-oil lamp or camphene lamp, 1840–1850. These lamps burned almost anything combustible, including cooking fats.

Bottom left: Pennsylvania arrowback chair with single plank seat. The painting and stenciling is most characteristic of the area, and is traditional in color and motif.

74

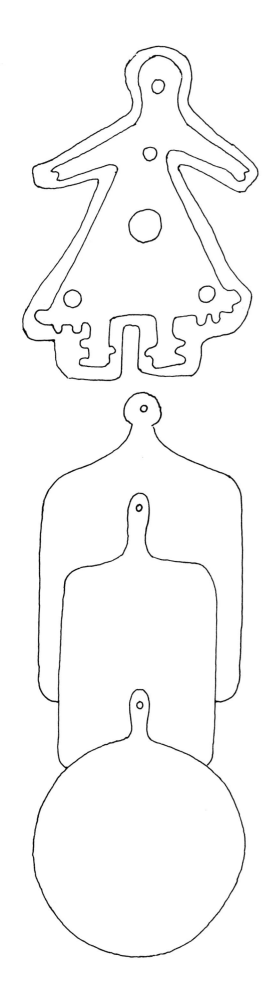

Top left: This little figure is one of many cookie-cutter shapes to be found in both New England and Pennsylvania.

Bottom left: Three noodle boards, averaging 24" in length and 1" in thickness. Boards are made of chestnut, walnut, beechwood, and pine.

Top right: Wrought-iron chopping knife. Single forged blade has turned-in ends to fasten blade to handle. Pennsylvania, 1800.

Center and bottom right: Wrought-iron kitchen utensils—forks, ladles, and flapjack shovel designs. Detail of riveted construction for added strength has little to do with the weight of the pancakes (we hope). The quantities of these primitive pieces still to be found in auctions testify to the volume of them produced by local blacksmiths in years past.

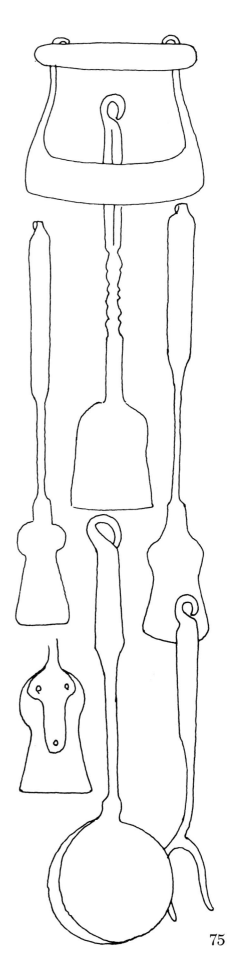

75

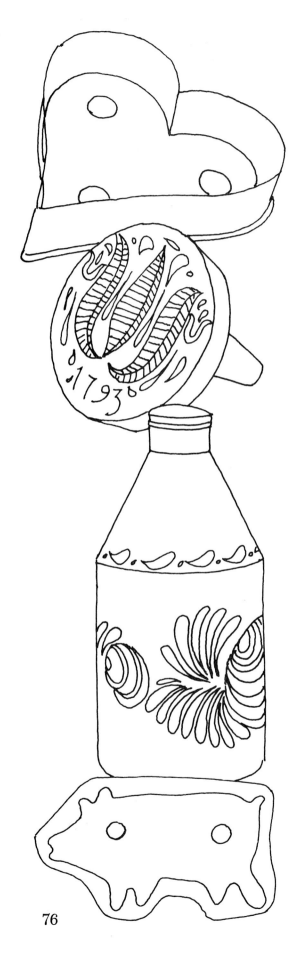

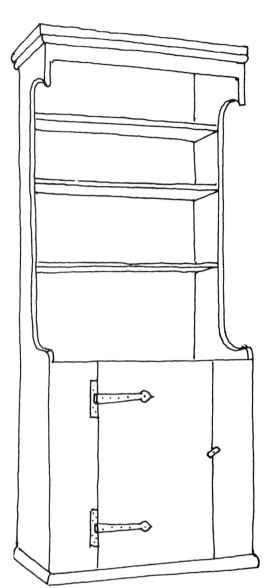

Top left: Heart-shaped pan, made of heavy tin. Large size indicates that it probably was made for a gingerbread baking mold.

Top right: Open pine cupboard with covered endboards has short arrowhead hinges of forged iron. Single-board door is primitive New England, early eighteenth century.

Upper left center: Butter mold of wood. Popular tulip design is typically Pennsylvania Dutch.

Lower left center: Decorated tin milk container. Designs are freehand-painted in black, red, and yellow.

Bottom left: Tin cooky cutter. These practical and decorative utensils are much sought after by both cooks and collectors.

Bottom right: Rye straw basket, made of heavy spiral twists woven together with thin strips of hickory. Baskets of this kind were used to store dried fruit.

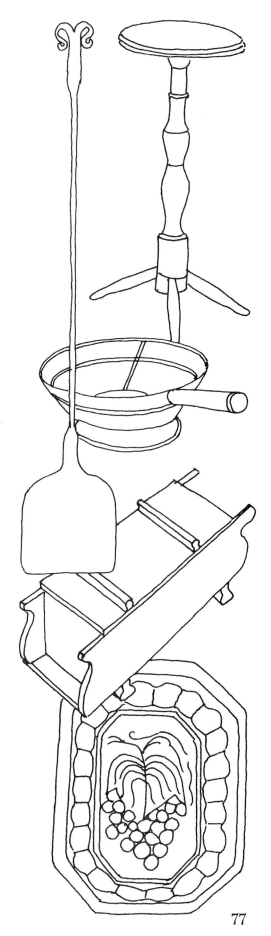

Top left: Two pressed-glass table lamps. Font of clear glass, decorated pottery and brass pedestal, blown-glass chimneys. These lamps were in mass production by the early 1800s.

Bottom left: Coffee pot and heater, painted tin. Nineteenth century. This interesting piece is probably one of the forerunners of the chafing dish. Cooking fats were probably used in flame container. (Philadelphia Museum of Art)

Top right: Dutch candle stand. Turning of maple, top pine. 1800s.

Upper right center: Heavy tin washbasin with dipper handle. Late nineteenth century. This dipper probably had a wooden handle as part of the tin handle.

Center right: Forged-iron oven shovel. These bread- or bean-pot oven shovels were also made of wood, for they were used only in the cooking processes.

Lower right center: Dough tray with handles for easier moving. Pennsylvania.

Bottom right: Salt-glazed earthenware mold with grape design. These deep-dish molds were used for desserts.

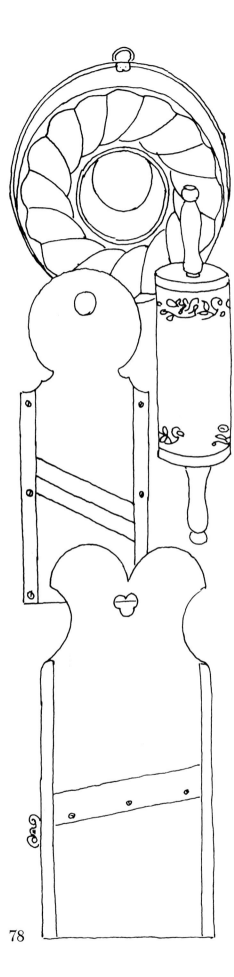

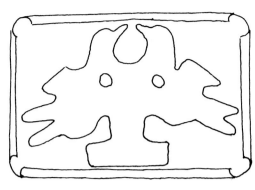

Top left: Deep, heavy tin cake mold, in the popular rope design of the Pennsylvania Dutch. This mold was also produced in heavy ceramic.

Center left: Salt-glaze Pennsylvania Dutch rolling pin. Handle can be unscrewed and ceramic cylinder filled with cold well water when rolling out dough.

Bottom left: Two Pennsylvania Dutch cabbage cutters made of walnut with forged knives. Slaw was an everyday staple and cutters are of sturdy construction for daily use.

Top right and lower right center: Tin cooky cutters were made both in New England and Pennsylvania. Practical for present use, these utensils of folk art are much sought after by collectors.

Upper center right: Decorated tin bread tray. Decal and freehand. Pennsylvania, 1750.

Bottom right: Rye straw basket with beaten ash handle, for gathering eggs.

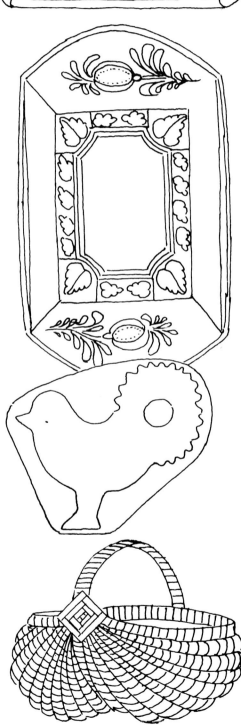

78

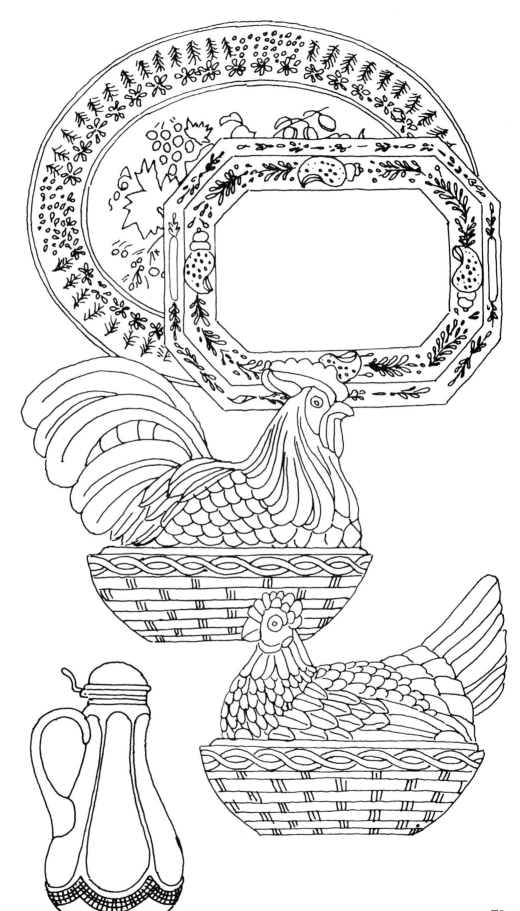

Top: Two painted tin trays. New England, 1820–1850. These painted trays are not to be confused with the Dutch toleware but were influenced by the English imports at that time.

Center: Pressed-glass rooster and hen. These interesting covered dishes were made in all sizes of clear glass with gilt painting, frosted glass, milk glass, and blue glass. Early Victorian. Said to have been used to serve soft- or hard-boiled eggs. As with many of these unique dishes, the uses were as varied as the users.

Bottom: Early syrup jug blown in a two-piece mold with pewter cap. New England, 1800s. Oddly, there was a great quantity of maple syrup made both in Ohio and Pennsylvania at that time and this jug was found in Pennsylvania.

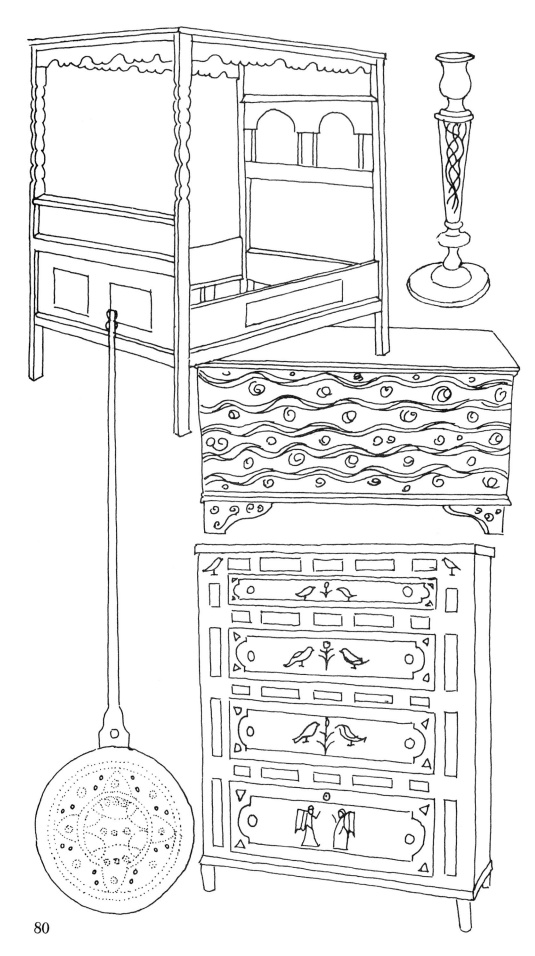

Top left: Decorated four-poster bed with stippling and feather-painted sunken panels, primitive flat cut posts. Pennsylvania Dutch, 1780s.

Bottom left: Brass, perforated and engraved warming pan with forged iron handle. Eighteenth century.

Top right: Tall blown candle stick. Column of shaft blown with a central air twist. Pittsburgh area, 1815–1830.

Center right: Small blanket chest boldly decorated with dry brush, sometimes called feather painting. Primitive.

Bottom right: Chest of drawers decorated with the conventional motifs of the Pennsylvania Dutch of 1820–1840. The differences in design indicate hand-painted decorations. (Philadelphia Museum of Art)

80

Auction Near Natchez

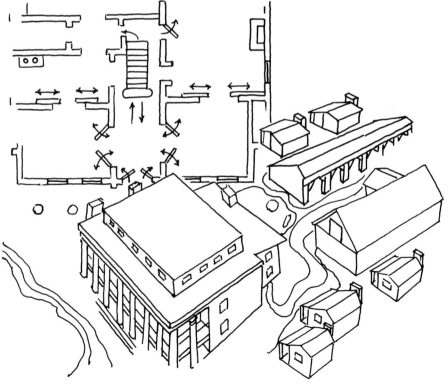

We started out early one summer morning and drove south along the Mississippi River. Our destination was the plantation Belle de Trudeau, on the east bank, some twelve or fourteen miles downriver. The rolling mist left the Mississippi's surface and slowly slid down the steep embankment of the levee and across the path of our car. The sun was shining somewhere, perhaps in a slightly brighter patch of fog to the east, but its light only made the thick fog in front of us more difficult to see through.

Maybe it was the chill of the heavy mist and the total wetness that made me so uncomfortable. But we both felt depressed, which was not usual for either of us, particularly when on our way to an auction. Perhaps it was just the prelude of another steaming Mississippi summer day.

The driving was slow and tedious. Fortunately, the distance was not far and we soon found the plantation entrance. It was close by the road, marked by two huge brick pillars topped with ball-type lights and a bronze sign indicating the plantation name and its present owner above the large lettering of the word "Private."

The plantation lay in an extremely low part of the country, and its acreage stretched some eight miles east from the Mississippi. How much river front the plantation included was not stated in the advertisement, for the property was not to be sold, at least on that day. The fog was heavier now and in that eerie light the distance from Natchez meant nothing—we might have been driving a million miles from nowhere.

As we continued along the spectacular oaklined entrance drive, we could see a small area in front of the plantation house. Its pillars looked very white and tall in the misty distance. Approaching the circle that brought us closer to the main entrance, we noticed a small group of people standing on the steps to the formal veranda. The people in the gathering looked undersized, for the enormous three-story columns and the deep, set-in windows seemed to dwarf everything.

The scene was ashen-gray. We parked our rented car alongside the other cars and walked toward the people grouped on the steps. Auctions were not new to us, but we were strangers here and would try to conform with the local behavior patterns. We naturally assumed that the people gathered on the steps were attending the auction. But somehow the feel of the place was different from previous auctions that we had attended, very different from the festive gatherings in New England or Pennsylvania. The people were very quiet here. There was none of the noisy chatter of neighbors brought together, and no covey of dealers feeling the undersides of chairs and tables or testing the ring of a glass object with a quick pencil tap. Nor was there any munching on hot dogs or sipping of soda pop. Everyone looked as if he shouldn't have been there at all. It was not going to be a gay day, I was sure—none of the usual fun and excitement of buying something you don't need and paying too much for it.

The mood was negative at Belle de Trudeau, and the heat and the Spanish moss hanging mournfully from the trees didn't help. As we moved closer to the main doorway, we were quite near the group that we had first seen when driving in. They were attired as if attending a formal garden party, and by listening to bits of their conversation, it became apparent that they were relatives, distant, but nevertheless, family. They seemed depressed by the legal arrangement that had given us access to their personal lives and their antiques.

The public proceeding seemed distasteful to them. Although we could see that there were a few outsiders beside ourselves, we sincerely wished we had more nonfamily company around us. The bids by the family were quietly indicated by unobtrusive hand gestures, and when one of their group had reached his limit of bidding, he simply turned his back on the auctioneer and returned to a quiet conversation in his particular circle.

The auctioneer in his morning coat and striped trousers did not add much to the atmosphere, for although he acknowledged bids with efficiency and aplomb, his demeanor was more that of a funeral director than one whose duty it was to gain as much revenue as possible for the estate. An air of gloom seemed to settle on everything and everyone. Buyers seemed to look upon their purchases with an air of disappointment, as if what they had just bought was an heirloom that had been passed on to them at the reading of the will, and now they were required to pay for it. And, at the same time, they were expected to mourn for the deceased in gratitude for the gift. In spite of the beautiful articles that came up for sale and the purchases for which we are still congratulating ourselves, we wished we had not come, for we felt a terrible sense of guilt.

Along the Mississippi River there is a feeling of both the heights of joy and the depths of great unhappiness. Sales, auctions, mortgages, loss of prestige as well as money are as much a part of almost every plantation as is the Spanish moss that drapes the trees. Sadly, the banks and other financial institutions are an integral part of these plantations. For the ebb and flow of economics is as constant as the rise of the Mississippi in the spring rush and its fall in dry autumn.

For the same reasons, many of the more valuable antiques and rare furnishings were removed to satisfy some of the financial obligations. The long years of attrition due to the Civil War surely took their toll. It is said that it would be impossible to evaluate the number of irreplaceable antiques and objects that were destroyed by fire and pillage during those years.

The story of the Belle de Trudeau plantation auction was compiled in such a way as not to embarrass any early families of the area. The name and locale have been altered so that the Natchez area could be included, for it is a repository of some of the greatest collections of early Americana to be found in this country.

It is virtually impossible to talk about the furnishings of these elegant houses along the Mississippi without some observations concerning these most unusual houses themselves. The evolution of the plantation culture and its earliest structures dates back to the early 1700s. Some are reputed to have been built even a century before this country's War of Independence. This surely places that area, its houses, and its furnishings, among the earliest of Americana to be gathered together anywhere. The great difference in this area of the county was its small pockets of great wealth and its relatively small society which was determined to live a most elegant life.

The earliest houses were built of local materials. The cottages were raised on pillars of brick, made from the clay of the river's banks, and coated with a coarse surfacing of mortar. The pillars supported the living areas high above the river's banks and the land's damp, rich earth. Fine cypress timber apparently could be taken from the swamp forests in endless quantities. Impervious to dampness and almost entirely resistant to any type of destructive force other than fire, this easy-to-work wood formed almost all the framing as well as some of the finely finished wood areas in the houses.

Virtually no stone originated in the delta region. When needed for either decorative or structural reasons, or simply as a whim of the builder, it had to be shipped from great distances. The lintels, mantels, and statuary that are found on many dwellings in the area were made of granite and marble that came from New England, Spain, Italy, and India. Some of the stone has been traced to South American sources.

It has been said by architectural experts that during the colonial period in the Mississippi delta there was a noticeable and distinct influence of West Indian structure and decor. However, a more moderate climate and a location not exposed to ocean winds and surf allowed for much larger and more sumptuously designed houses. These modifications in original West Indian designs, along with influences from other places, created a charming synthesis of Greek Revival or Creole Classic, a unique composite found nowhere else in the world.

Victorianism reached into the gulf states in the late 1850s, as everywhere else, and projected its influence. The Gothic influence was later added to the architectural mix, producing the quaint Steamboat Gothic. This charming form of architecture can still be found in parts of the delta area. The colonial North left its mark on Georgian styles and, if it is not apparent in the exterior of these river houses, it is certainly recognizable in the interior floor plans. The huge central halls, flanked by square rooms on either side and repeated on the second level of the house, differ very little from their Georgian counterparts in Virginia and Maryland. In some cases, the stairs were laid on the exterior rather than in the center hall, which was, of course, a major departure from the authentic Georgian style. The roofs were another departure from Georgian styles, and were dictated by weather concerns.

Surprisingly, only a small area of land was cleared around the river plantation. Other than the expansiveness of the grand entrance driveway, which framed the main house, there was little cleared land around the carriage houses and slaves' quarters, and the food storage barns were built quite close to the main house. There was a great formal garden leading to the front colonnade of the house with an impressive row of huge and ancient oaks, draped with streamers of Spanish moss.

Unfortunately, the wealth of the affluent river society was dependent on two basic commodities: cotton, the king from 1800 to 1850, and then the sugar market from 1825 to 1875. It was during that relatively limited period that American art and furnishings accumulated in this area of the South. Many of the antiques were French, Spanish, and Italian in origin. What was not purchased in New Orleans or Baton Rouge seemed to come from southern Europe. A few pieces, however, showed the influence of the English and the elegance of Virginia Colonial furniture, but none of the antiques carried the distinct look of primitive New England. The woods were generally mahogany and rosewood.

The affluence of this short-lived era came to an abrupt end with the freeing of the slaves at the end of the Civil War. The industrialization of the American economy that followed soon afterward produced the final changes. The river society never recovered from these economic blows.

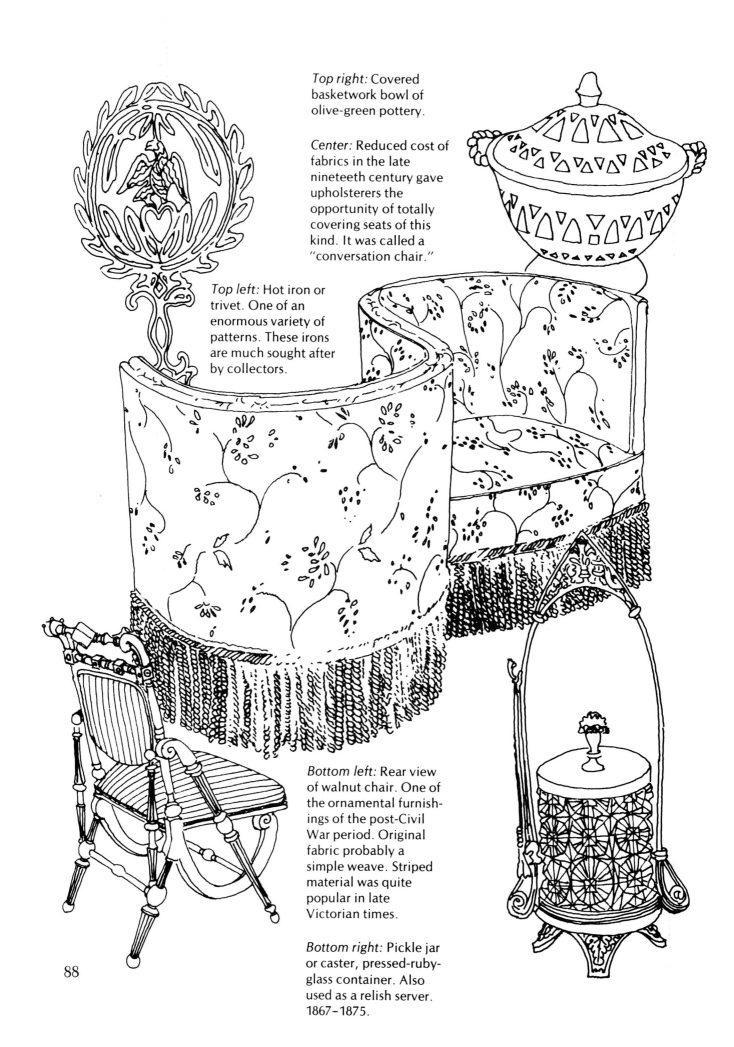

Top right: Covered basketwork bowl of olive-green pottery.

Center: Reduced cost of fabrics in the late nineteeth century gave upholsterers the opportunity of totally covering seats of this kind. It was called a "conversation chair."

Top left: Hot iron or trivet. One of an enormous variety of patterns. These irons are much sought after by collectors.

Bottom left: Rear view of walnut chair. One of the ornamental furnishings of the post-Civil War period. Original fabric probably a simple weave. Striped material was quite popular in late Victorian times.

Bottom right: Pickle jar or caster, pressed-ruby-glass container. Also used as a relish server. 1867–1875.

Top : Eight-foot
secretary, document
drawer with finials.
Decorative urns, spiral
carvings, shell carvings.
Early eighteenth
century. This secretary
was about as efficient
as anything short of a
private office.
Undoubtedly built to a
businessman's specifi-
cations.

Bottom left: Quart-
capacity decanter
patterned in
three-piece mold. Clear
light-green glass.
Nonlead. Middle
eastern. Could be a
Boston and Sandwich
Glass Company piece.
Probably Ohio area.
1830–1840.

Bottom center: Free-
blown sugar bowl,
galleried rim, clear lead
glass. Copper-wheel
engraving typical of
Pittsburgh area glass,
early 1800s.

Bottom right: Quarter-
pint decanter. Three-
piece mold, clear lead
glass. Ribbed wheel
stopper. Sandwich,
1840.

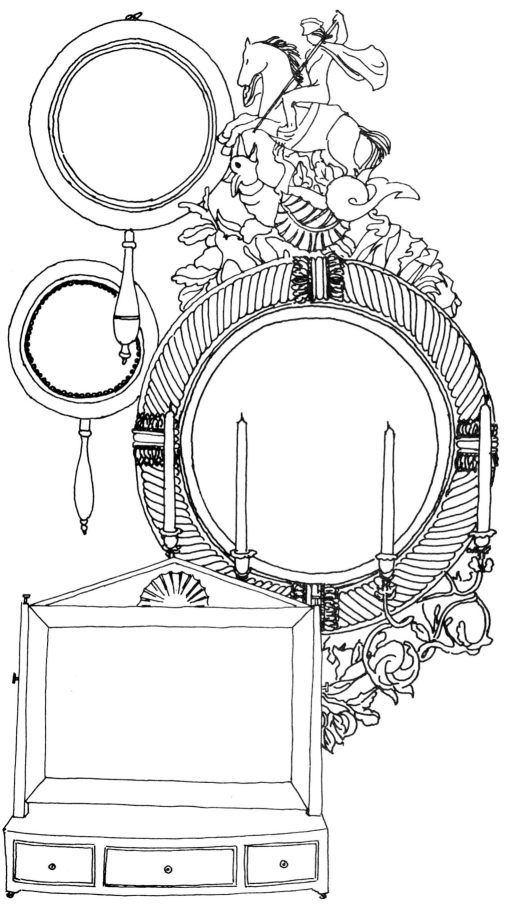

Top left: Two simple wood-framed hand mirrors. Simple, attractive design, walnutwood handles.

Top right: Extremely large and ornate girandole, depicting St. George and the dragon. The convex mirror radiates the candlelight in all directions. Very early nineteenth century. These very ornate pieces had a very definite Southern European influence. With the affluent market in the delta area and the Spanish and French background of some families of influence, these ornate pieces found a great deal of acceptance in the gulf states.

Bottom: Hepplewhite, mahogany shaving glass. Early eighteenth century. Inlaid fan is single ornament to the beautiful simplicity of the tasteful piece.

Top: Carved and gilded half-spindle Empire mirror.

Center: Entertaining and extremely rare China-trade porcelain hand holding a brass urn-shaped candle holder. 1780. What with ships stopping along the gulf coast before their long journey around Cape Horn to San Francisco, furnishings and articles of decoration were being circulated along the entire gulf seaboard. No longer were pieces from far-off places unavailable. Ships returned from the West Coast with art objects brought to that coast by the China trade. South American articles, ideas, and objects also found themselves in this Mississippi area.

Bottom: Field bed was so called because its canopy top suggested a "tent." Mahogany. Pressed brass cover for bolt holes. Late eighteenth century.

91

Top left: Carved rosewood chair made by John Henry Belter of New York. Mid-1800s. Belter's unique designing was and still is most popular.

Center left: Chair with reed seat made of turned imitation bamboo, probably of maple. 1875. Bamboo was popularized by the Caribbean influences and reached its height of style in the late Victorian era.

Bottom left: Hitchcock chair with rush seat, sometimes called "pillowback." Middle 1800s. An extremely comfortable and popular design, it was sometimes painted and decorated.

Top right: Wicker platform rocker. Probably made on the East Coast about 1850. This wicker influence came from almost everywhere: Africa, India, the Caribbean. Its popularity was due mainly to the porch, then being constructed on almost every private house and most public ones.

Lower right: Tufted, overstuffed chair. Fringe is of pure silk as is the material of the entire chair. Late Victorian. Very few of these large pieces are still in existence. What with the deterioration of the upholstery fabric and the stuffing they were likely to fall apart in a very few years.

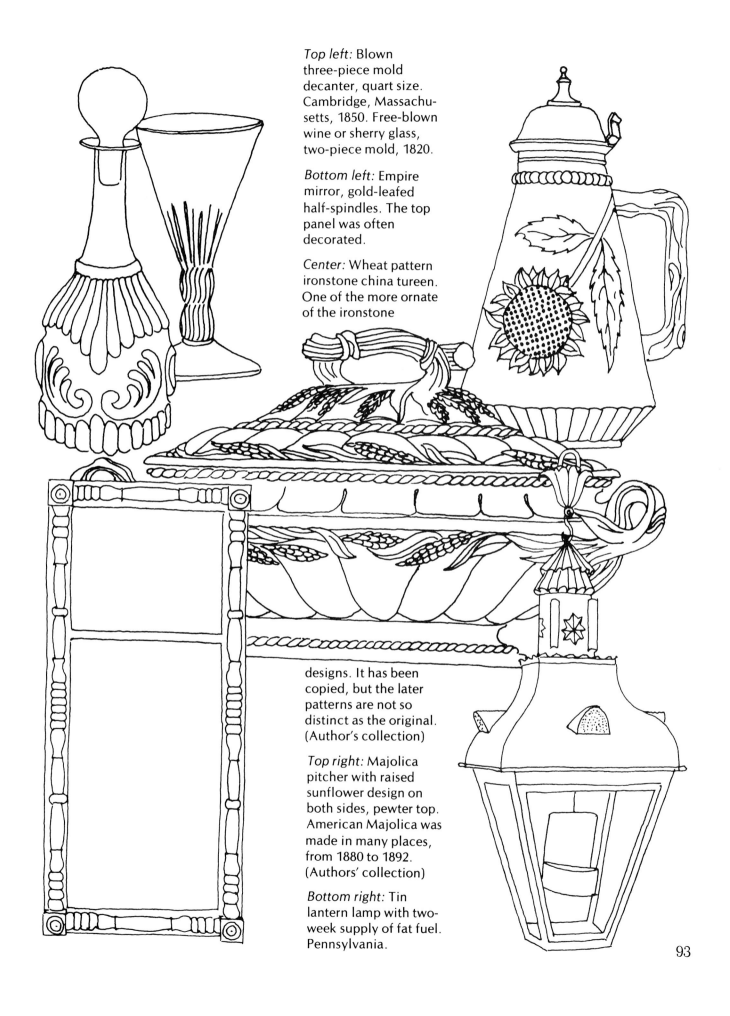

Top left: Blown three-piece mold decanter, quart size. Cambridge, Massachusetts, 1850. Free-blown wine or sherry glass, two-piece mold, 1820.

Bottom left: Empire mirror, gold-leafed half-spindles. The top panel was often decorated.

Center: Wheat pattern ironstone china tureen. One of the more ornate of the ironstone designs. It has been copied, but the later patterns are not so distinct as the original. (Author's collection)

Top right: Majolica pitcher with raised sunflower design on both sides, pewter top. American Majolica was made in many places, from 1880 to 1892. (Authors' collection)

Bottom right: Tin lantern lamp with two-week supply of fat fuel. Pennsylvania.

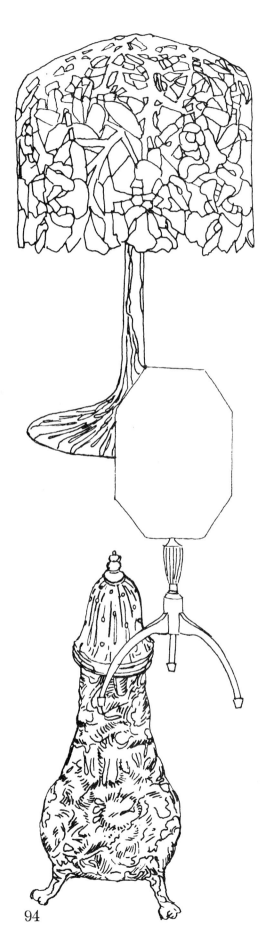

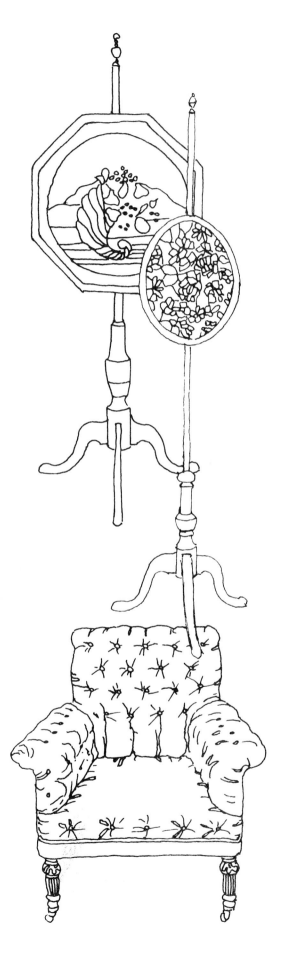

Top left: Tiffany lampshade. Trumpet-flower design. Late nineteenth century with cast bronze base. These ornate lamps have enjoyed a revival in the last few years and are so popular as to be overpriced. Much care must be taken to identify an original from a copy.

Center left: Hepplewhite tilt-top table with spade feet. 1790–1810. These charming small or occasional tables are harder to come by as the years go on, for they seem to fit anywhere and are highly prized by their owners.

Bottom left: Silver salt. Late 1800s. Made by eastern silversmiths. Ornate design was the direction at that time. Contrary to earlier work, silversmiths seemed to feel that the entire area had to be covered with design forms.

Top right: Two mahogany fire screens with needlepoint floral designs. Newport, 1750–1760.

Bottom right: Deeply upholstered armchair. Fabric covering. Late Victorian. This is typical of the comfort-comes-first era. The lines are reasonably good, but the overstuffed look cared little for that.

94

Top left: Blown and cut pitcher, clear lead glass, four large blocks of strawberry diamonds separated by a single pillar. Star cutting on base. 1840.

Center left: Free-blown wineglass. Aquamarine, nonlead. 1800s.

Top right: Sandwich bottle stopper with floral design composed of Millefiori center. Petals are of red with white striping and dotted with gold stone. Dewdrops made of tiny bubbles.

Center right: Blown compote on standard. Clear lead glass. Copper wheel engraving with leaf and petaled flower design. North-central United States, 1840–1860.

Bottom right: Colonial brass andirons, ball-and-baluster pattern on splayed feet.

Top and center left: Two small heavy silver mugs with handsome scroll handles, molded rim, and folded flaring foot. Attributed to Benjamin Burt, Silversmith, Boston, early 1800s.

Bottom left: Queen Anne tilt-top table, mahogany. 1750.

Top right: Four-drawer Queen Anne lowboy with scrolled skirt and graceful legs. 1740.

Center: Veneered mahogany bed in the French Empire style. Often referred to as a "sleigh bed." Popular after 1820.

Bottom right: Queen Anne walnut chest of drawers and wardrobe, brass fittings. 1750–1770. The wardrobe was an essential furnishing for the bedroom in most early houses. Closets are a relatively modern architectural innovation and did not appear in house plans until late Victorian times.

Top right: Table lamps of this kind were in great supply by most mail order houses and the local general store. The pressed-glass font came in a variety of designs and colors and was interchangeable with a variety of bases. Some bases were porcelain or pressed glass. The clear glass ones were for personalized decorating, either painting or filling with colorful dried flowers. Middle 1800s.

Center: Maple table of simulated bamboo. An extremely popular style of furniture in the late 1800s. Beds, tables, chairs, practically everything to furnish the house was made in this unique style.

Top left: Pier table of mahogany veneer in the style of Meeks and Hall. Late Victorian. These were usually used as hall pieces.

Bottom left: Salt glaze stoneware pitcher. The gray-white glaze gives this ware a truly elegant look. Patterns on stoneware were in bas-relief and depicted all types of subjects.

97

Top left: A "still" bank which followed the ingenious animated banks. These still banks were made in quantity following the Civil War period.

Bottom left: Pine lantern with hollowed-out top and perforated tin cap.

Top right: Trick pony bank. The coin is deposited in the pony's mouth. When lever at back is pulled out, the pony's neck bends down and the coin drops into the feed trough.

Bottom right: Duncan Phyfe tambour sewing table with vase-shaped pedestal and brass lion-paw feet. Early Victorian. Often referred to as a "lady helper."

Bottom: Blown three-mold covered dish on a plate. Domed cover and large folding rim, heavy finial. 1825–1850.

TRICK PONY

The Barkers'
Sale in Dallas

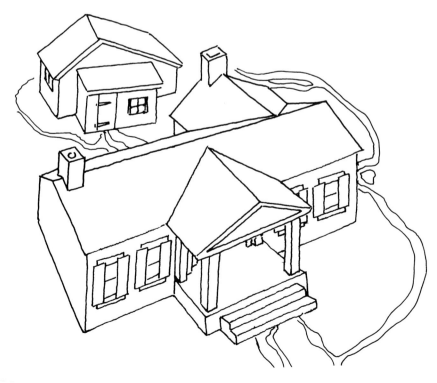

There was a lot of excitement at the ranch that morning for the newly married couple. The Barkers' shipment of furnishings had arrived in Dallas, and the crates would have to be picked up at the Texas and Pacific Railroad station. Jeff hitched up a team and he and his wife started in for the wagonload of boxes they knew would be on the freight platform. The young couple talked all the way, of how their furnishings would look, where they would put the pieces, and how great it would be to finally have some of the household necessities that they had done without for so long.

Jeff talked about his first trip on the railroad to the gulf port. It had been quite a few years before—1863, he recalled—in celebration of the completion of the track to Dallas. Now, over ten years later, he was happily married, and all was well on the ranch, both with their cattle and with their crops.

His cotton had yielded a surprising crop; almost three times the expected baleage per acre. The price was high, for all the nation seemed to need cotton, since some of the south-central cotton fields were still not in full production. Texas cotton, Texas rice, and Texas onions were fetching high prices and the Barkers were receiving their just share. The trip he and his wife had made to Shreveport to sell their produce and to purchase their furnishings had, indeed, been both business and pleasure. It had also been the Barkers' honeymoon.

The bride of just a few months could now decorate the ranch house in comfort with some of the familiar furnishings she remembered growing up with in her parents' house in southern Illinois. The old homestead seemed a long way off now, but in reality she and Jeff had practically grown up together, and she had come to join him just as soon as he was settled and capable of taking care of her.

Some of the items that they had bought in Shreveport might look a bit strange in their rugged ranch house, but Jeff was bound to do better and what they had bought would look elegant in a Dallas town house.

There was little choice of style in the Shreveport stores, furniture looked sort of French and Spanish. They bought some of their things in second-hand stores. There were very few of the plain wood pieces of furniture the Barkers remembered so well at home in the North—beds of maple wood, pine chests, and wide board tables of chestnut or oak. In any case, the articles of their choice would add color and comfort to their new home. The polished and upholstered pieces would brighten the rooms of rough planking, and the new curtains would contribute even more color. It was, after all, just a beginning for them.

Fortunately, the recorded history of the southwestern part of our country has been well kept by dedicated and thoughtful men. Although their records are sparse in words, what they put down on paper is informative: the color of the times and the hard facts of colonization.

There are early documents that recorded the settling of small groups of people in and around the lower, coastal part of Texas in the 1820s. The earliest settlements were peopled by restless souls from states bordering Texas to the east. In and around what is now known as Austin, Texas, is a record of a settlement dating about 1822. The date of this settlement was closely followed by a group called DeWitt's Colony, which homesteaded quite near the Austin group. The records are rather vague as to how many people settled there, but the DeWitt colonization seems to have been started in or about 1825. The populating of Texas continued, with small groups settling in isolated areas at a rather steady pace until 1836. The settlements worked togther for the same objective, and Texas eventually won her independence.

An early record shows that the original pioneer families of Dallas County totaled less than 1500 people, including the children. With little to offer except large areas of brushland, the new population expected little and was drawn from the states and territories to the east. However, a few of the hardy settlers came from states as far away as Missouri, Illinois, Ohio, and parts of western Pennsylvania. Some wagon trains arrived from the Virginia coast, which, at that time, meant a long and dangerous journey. To get to Texas, one had to really want to go there, since wagon trains traveling westward did not normally pass through there. It did not offer the glamor of finding gold, a perfect climate, perfect harbors, deep tillable soil, commerce with other parts of the world, or great natural resources. It seemed to offer the people who settled there some intangible that they apparently needed and were willing to work for. Whatever it was, it welded them all into a culture distinctly their own.

When the father of Dallas, John Neely Bryan, a settler from Tennessee, plotted out the first known map of the town of Dallas, it was late in the year 1846. The town's first house, a log cabin, stood on what is now Broadway, between Main and Commerce streets. John Neely Bryan's original plan continued as the basic plan of expansion until 1856, twenty years after Texas had become a republic and the city of Dallas had been created by an act of the Texas legislature. And, it was John Neely Bryan's friendship and admiration for George Mifflin Dallas, vice-president of the United States during the Polk administration, that resulted in the naming of both the county and the city.

The population of Dallas continued to grow, and the future of the area seemed bright. The first official United States census, completed in 1860, showed a population of over 775 persons within the Dallas city limits and indicated a few additional families in outlying areas.

When in 1861 Texas joined the cause for the South, it did as all the southern states did—seceded from the Union. The losses of men and materiel to that cause were what few states could afford—Texas, with its small population, probably least of all. But the will of the Texan came through at the end of the War of the States; new building and the development of industry was again on its way. Dallas began to expand her city lines to accommodate a fast-increasing population.

When the Texas Central Railway added track to include Dallas, it relieved an overburdened water transportation system, until then the only method of moving heavy freight. Dallas soon had alternate routes to the gulf ports, and the more adventuresome people from those ports began to move inland. A few years later, the Texas and Pacific Railroad reached into the outskirts of Dallas. The expanding city accommodated a rising population and changing needs. The people of Dallas built one of the earliest libraries in the entire Southwest. Their remoteness for so many years made them hunger for entertainment, so they also built one of the earliest opera houses in the area.

This expansiveness, so typical of Texans, coupled with an influx of visitors, salesmen, and adventurers, brought about a need for transient accommodations, and so the impressive Empire Hotel was built. This monument of hospitality was finally replaced by an even grander hostelry some six years later, in 1869. The newly completed Windsor Hotel merged with its next-door neighbor, the LaGrande Hotel, to become the Grand Windsor Hotel, surpassing any hotel in Texas, both in size and in its luxurious Victorian accommodations.

It was quite natural that good business would follow this kind of expansiveness. Dallas became the forerunner of intraterritory business and its firms began to seek out firms as far away as Houston, 275 miles below, and Shreveport, 200 miles to the southeast.

Commerce with other states was bound to bring in articles of luxury and beauty to add to people's comfort. The hotels were probably the first showcases of the luxurious Victorian mode of living. The Texans caught on fast and wanted the same kind of comfort. So the importation of Victorian Americana, along with articles of the antebellum period, began in Dallas. Huge plantations in southern states were breaking up, and the people of Dallas not only had the money to pay for the lavish furnishings that were created prior to the Civil War, but also had the means of transporting the costly articles. In a similar manner, fine collections of Victorian furnishings were purchased for the better homes of early Dallas.

The rapid expansion of the hotel business in Dallas was a major influence on the Barkers and their life-style. By that time, Jeff Barker was supplying beef and general produce to most of the hotels in the Dallas area, and for this reason was in almost daily contact with their various managements. It was only natural that the newer hotels would attract the Dallas visitors and that smaller establishments would be forced out of business, either for lack of competitive accommodations or for other reasons leading to a decline in their popularity. In any case, several of them were closed and the furnishings that filled their rooms were sold either privately or at public auction to satisfy their owners' debts.

The items that furnished the better hotels were generally mass produced and of commercial quality, which was true of almost all furnishings and decorative items manufactured during that particular growth period of our history. Sandwich glass was mass produced and was also used for commercial packaging; Hitchcock chairs were made in three separate factories; and hardly a clock came out of New England that wasn't one of thousands of identical design. Even in those early times the few individually made pieces of Americana were hard to come by. However, the better rooms in even the smallest of these hotels did contain some decorative pieces that were both classic and valuable. Double-globe lamps—now referred to as "Gone with the Wind" lamps—in a variety of shapes and colors; settees of questionable comfort, chests of drawers painted with oak striping or bird's-eye maple designs to cover their pine or solid walnut construction; occasional tables; mirrors with carved and gold-leaf frames; and a seemingly limitless quantity of glassware from the inevitable hotel bar—all these appeared and were offered for sale. This sudden deluge of furnishings loosed on the people of Dallas were further increased by yet another activity of those changing times. The sharp competition for customers that existed among the new and large hotels necessitated the constant updating and modernizing of their most expensive suites. The turnover in the decorating fashions was as endless as the news of style changes that came from the cities in the East.

The influence of these hotels, their transient visitors, the opera house and its entertainers on the life-style of the residents of Dallas could not be overestimated and the Barkers were certainly no exception. Their Illinois upbringing, along with their years in Texas, allowed them to enjoy and collect items with little regard for the origin of their design or manufacture. Jeff Barker's intimate knowledge of the internal business operations of most of these hotels gave him a most important advantage in purchasing what he liked—a timely opportunity, as he and his wife were about to furnish their newly acquired home.

The Barkers' property, once outside the Dallas city lines, was now well within the limits of the burgeoning metropolis and, accordingly, had increased in value. What Jeff Barker had not earned on the ranch was more than compensated for by its real estate value, and the house in town he had promised his bride many years before had become a reality. The original furnishings that they bought on their honeymoon trip to Shreveport had been added to with more luxurious pieces, some early, some Victorian, but the earlier pieces of Texas antiquity they had held, for this was where it had all begun for them.

Added to that, of course, were the quantities of furnishings and bric-a-brac the Barkers had bought during the business expansion period in Dallas. Then there was the collection that was so much a part of Jeff's early start in Texas—pre-Civil War firearms; arrowheads, Indian work tools of unusual design and quality; beadwork and leatherwork, including harnesses and saddles. The huge freight wagon he had kept in a barn he gave to a neighboring rancher. As time went on some of his silver-mounted saddles were exchanged with friends for early firearms, to supplement his already-large collection. An old friendship and a swap effected a transaction that money could not have hoped to do. The one-story town house they were about to furnish could not possibly hold the quantity of possessions they had accumulated. So, with great care, they selected all the pieces they could not bear to part with, either sold or gave away the rest, and moved into the small house with the lovely front yard on a street right in the center of the busy town of Dallas.

The furnishings and objects of early America, brought together so many years before by the love and interest of the Barkers, were now to be disbursed. Some pieces were left by the Barkers to the city's museum, where they rightfully belonged, and the rest will be found in the homes of collectors and buyers, where it is hoped that they will be cherished as reminders of early Texas history.

Top left: Scroll or violin flask, free-blown into two-piece mold, dark-green lead glass. New England, 1850.

Bottom left: Fine Queen Anne highboy with shell motif carvings, brass pulls.

Top right: Unique eagle or duckbill pattern ironstone cocoa pot, marked Imperial White Granite, Gelson Brothers, Hanley, England.

Center right: One of a pair of copper-luster-on-white porcelain Staffordshire spaniels. These entertaining and decorative pieces were copied in many different ways.

Bottom right: Wrought-iron pastry wheel. (Metropolitan Museum)

106

Top: Three-part Sheraton table, reeded legs. This large table is of solid mahogany. Casters and brass sockets are fitted to end of each leg post.

Center left: Horn chair made in Massillon, Ohio. Upholstered with flowered damask and fitted with cloven-hoofed feet. Late Victorian.

Center right and bottom left: Three flasks shown are all of nonlead glass, flattened ovoid shape, and free-blown into molds of various designs.

Bottom right: Tip-and-turn table, carved bowl and fluted shaft. Solid mahogany. Piecrust top. 1760–1775.

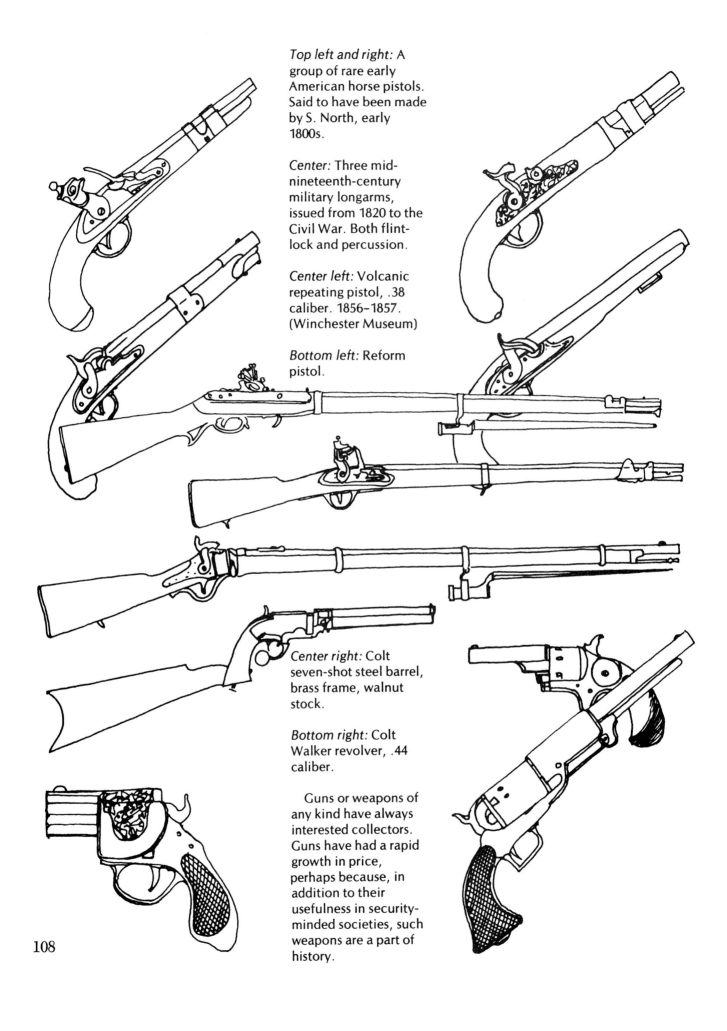

Top left and right: A group of rare early American horse pistols. Said to have been made by S. North, early 1800s.

Center: Three mid-nineteenth-century military longarms, issued from 1820 to the Civil War. Both flint-lock and percussion.

Center left: Volcanic repeating pistol, .38 caliber. 1856–1857. (Winchester Museum)

Bottom left: Reform pistol.

Center right: Colt seven-shot steel barrel, brass frame, walnut stock.

Bottom right: Colt Walker revolver, .44 caliber.

Guns or weapons of any kind have always interested collectors. Guns have had a rapid growth in price, perhaps because, in addition to their usefulness in security-minded societies, such weapons are a part of history.

Top left and bottom right: The four salts shown are Stiegel-type and midwestern. These were made in quantity by the bottle factories and preceded the pressed glass salts.

Left: The rare lighthouse clock. Most sought after of antique clocks.

Top right: Walnut wood upholstered wing chair of the early Queen Anne period. These chairs are much sought after for their practical comfort as well as their antique value.

Center right: Handsome mirror with attractive mahogany frame in the style of the Queen Anne period. Early 1700s.

109

Top left: Eagle-splatted rush-seated Hitchcock side chair. Late Sheraton design. The splat is carved and stenciled to represent an eagle surmounting a terrestrial globe. 1820.

Center left: Pressed-glass syrup pitcher with pewter top. Mid-Victorian. Free-blown into three-piece mold.

Bottom left: Two styles of hexagonal brass andirons. 1800s. These attractive irons were particularly extravagant, and probably used for a living room fireplace.

Top right: Two brass-eagle door knockers; one brass knocker of more conventional design. Nineteenth century.

Bottom right: Dunce-cap stove was patented in Poughkeepsie in 1816. Conical iron cap was made to radiate additional heat. The built-in fender, the collar under the cap, and the finials are all of brass.

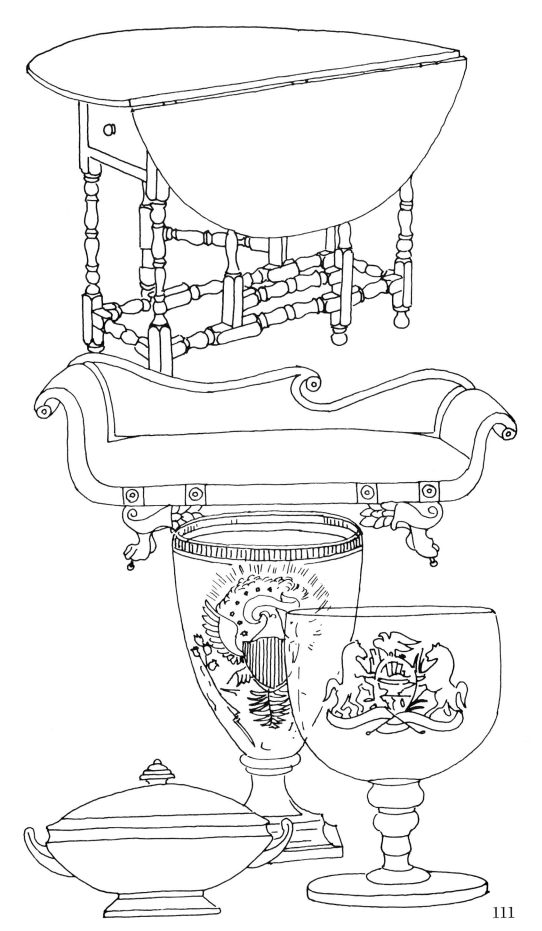

Top: Turned maple and pine gateleg table. Middle 1700s.

Center: American Empire cornucopia settee. These interesting pieces often incorporate ormolu in the wood-frame designs.

Bottom right: Goblet of nonlead glass, six-point cut star on bottom of foot. Goblet with copper-wheel engraving of eagle and banner bearing legend E PLURIBUS UNUM. (Henry Francis du Pont, Winterthur Museum) The date of these goblets is highly speculative. Detail indicates them to be made in the late 1790s, probably by an eastern glass works.

Bottom left: Ironstone tureen. These undecorated tureens were in great supply in Victorian times. Made at many pottery works all through the East and Midwest.

111

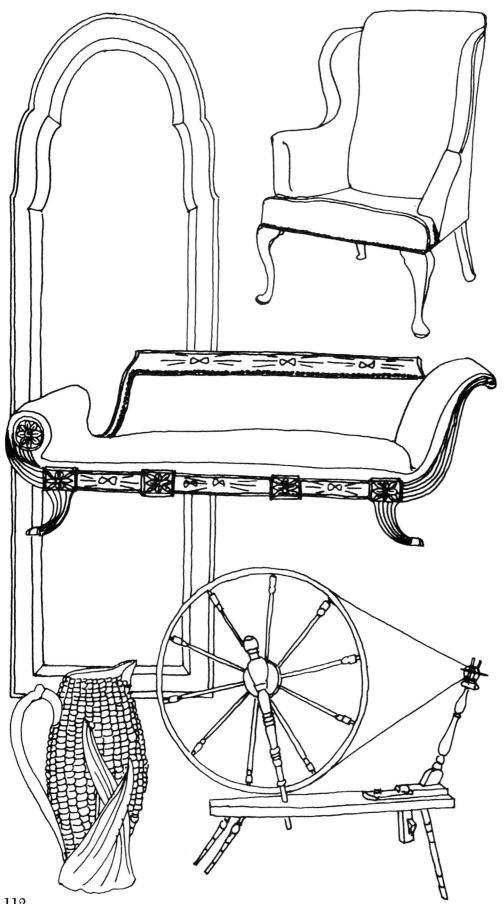

Left: Full-length mirror, Queen Anne type. Walnut veneer. These heavy long mirrors were much prized, particularly the beveled kind.

Bottom left: Small Majolica pitcher, raised corncob design. American Majolica was made in Baltimore, Trenton, Ohio, New York, and New Hampshire, from 1880 to 1900.

Top right: Queen Anne. Probably one of the most comfortable of the high-back chairs, as well as one of the most attractive. Note: no separate seat cushion.

Center: Duncan Phyfe sofa, carved and reeded ends and legs. Covered in original black horsehair, early 1800s.

Bottom right: Large spinning wheel was used in the first step to form thread of the raw cotton.

112

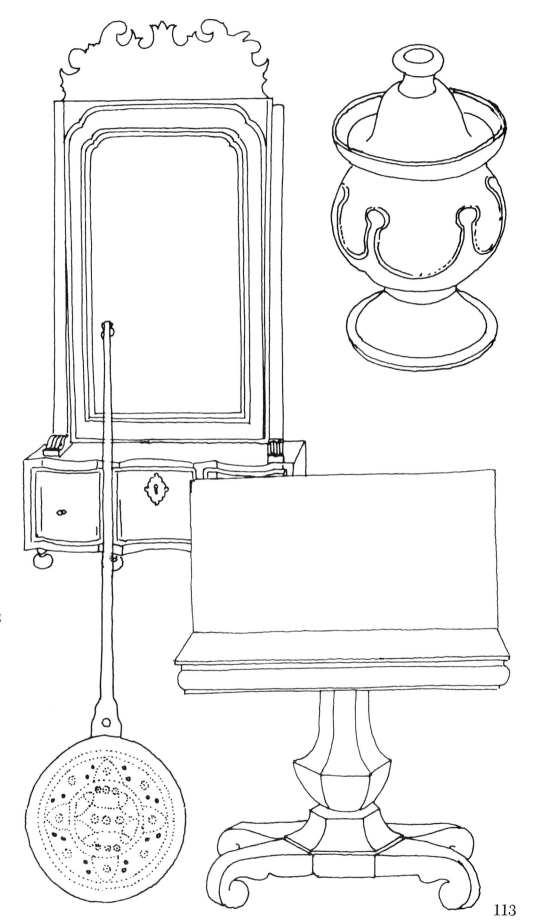

Top left: Shaving glass, light walnut wood, probably New England. Pine is used on the internal structure. Very early construction.

Bottom left: Eighteenth-century perforated and engraved brass warming pan with forged iron handle.

Top right: Free-blown sugar bowl with overlay lily-pad design, characteristic of New York glass houses, 1830–1875 period.

Bottom right: Card table with drop or folding top. Flame mahogany with veneer base over pine. Closely related to designs by Meeks and Hall.

113

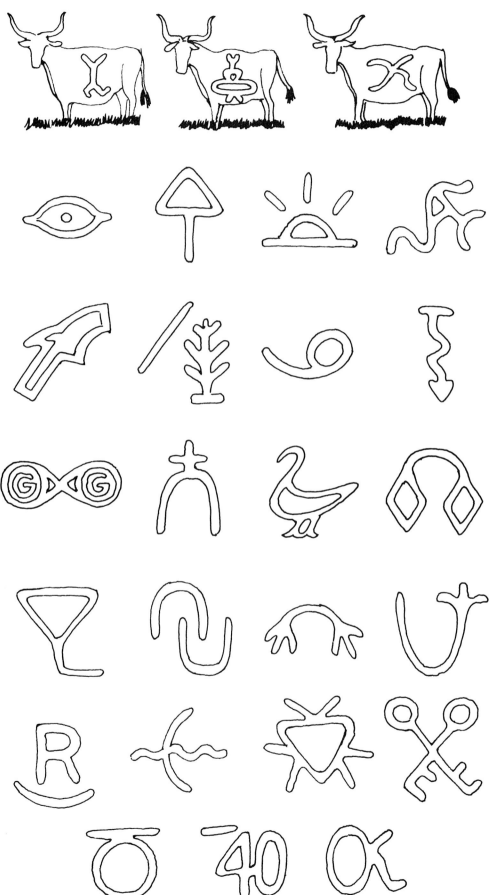

Branding irons. *Reading top row from left to right:* Walking-Y, Old Woman, Windflower, Pig's Eye, Pine Tree, Rising Sun, Running Sack, Six-Shooter, Slash Pine, Sleeping Six, Bent Arrow, Spectacle-G, Spur, Swan, Swinging Diamonds, Triangle Trail, Tumbling Horseshoes, Turkey Track, U-Fly, Rocking-R, Snake-in-Moon, Triangle-X, Walking Tadpole, Hanging O, Bar Forty, and OK.

Brands are now registered like copyrights or trademarks, but in those early days the blacksmith's inventiveness was all that protected each rancher's brand.

It is interesting that in today's modern marketplace manufacturers are extremely protective of their "brands."

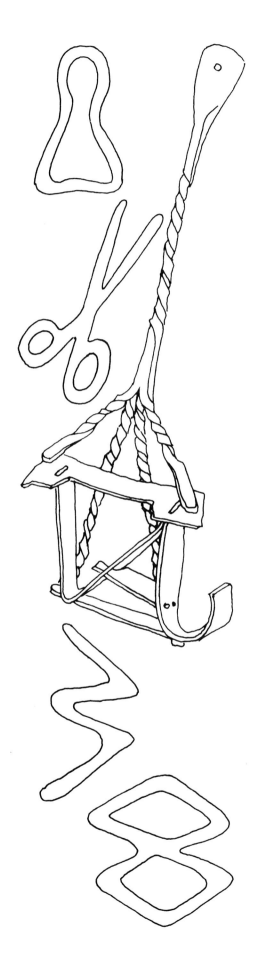

The beautifully forged branding iron on the left is from the collection of Robert W. Loughlin and is the Lazy JA brand.

Left top to bottom, the brand diagrams are: Keyhole, Scissors, and at bottom the Lazy-M, which was a fine prerustler brand that lent itself perfectly to the stealing of cattle, since the Lazy-M could easily be changed into the Twin Diamond brand. The Twin-Diamond was the "noose" result.

Right top to bottom: Slashed Lazy S, Cloudy Moon, Hat Brand (designed in many styles), Triangle B, Safety Pin, Saddle Horn, and Texas Barbeque.

The designs of brands seem endless, for the truth is that they are continually being originated for all sorts of purposes. Those collectors who confine themselves to collecting the actual irons are more likely to be able to separate the old from the new.

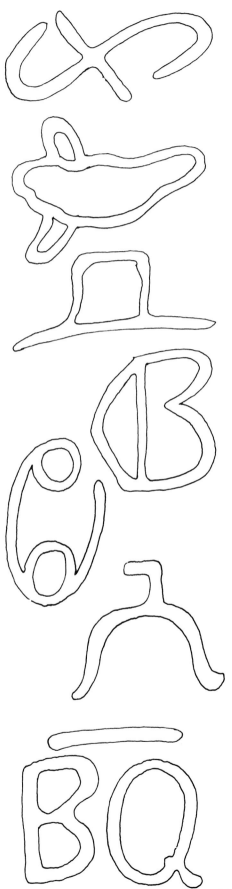

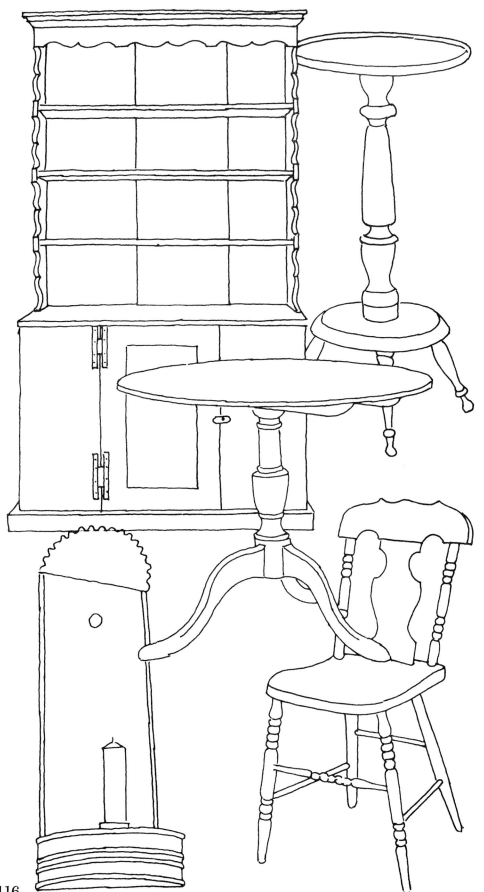

Top left: Open-shelved pine dresser with "H" hinges, a primitive piece. "Dunker" in its simplicity. Door at base usually not paneled.

Bottom left: Early tin sconce. This is of the pressed-tin style. Probably earlier than punched-tin designs.

Top right: Candlestand. Turned pedestal of maple. 1780.

Center: Tilt-top table. Pedestal of rock maple, top board pine. This same style of table can be found in mahogany. 1750–1770.

Bottom right: This plank seat chair is of the 1850s period. Abraham Lincoln was said to have had six of these prior to his departure for Washington, D.C., in 1861.

The Auction
Near Abilene,
Kansas

The year was 1868, when Virginia and Matthew V. Loughlin jounced about on the springless driver's seat of their oversized freight wagon on their way to Abilene, Kansas. For almost two months they had been traveling north on the Chisholm Trail, first from Galveston, then through Austin. Another half month was spent on the trail's extension up into Kansas. The passage through the Indian teritory had been uneventful despite the frightening tales of cowhands who had joined them part of the way. Their wagon train had followed droves of longhorns north, herds so large that they seemed countless and covered the plain with a seemingly endless blanket of hair and hide, yet just some of the many herds that would be driven through Texas to Abilene and the McCoy pens that stretched along the tracks of the Pacific and Kansas Railroad. News of the expanding market in beef in the East and a land of opportunity in Abilene had reached the Loughlins in Galveston. Their tiny general store was struggling in its day-to-day business, and Matthew's longing for the security of farming would never be satisfied in the hot and dry gulf town of Galveston.

Stories of the deep black soil of Kansas at the end of the Chisholm, practically for the asking, urged them to pack the salable items from their store and convert the rest of their holdings into a freight wagon and make their way north, into Kansas, and a brand-new life.

History tells us that the prairie country west of Topeka, Kansas, was practically empty of inhabitants through the 1860s. At that time there were only a few rugged souls in the whole of huge Kansas state. The pioneers, who gave little thought to the coyotes, gray wolves, and rattle-snakes, were more concerned with the strong winds that blew constantly across the endless rolling plains. The Kansas plains were covered with buffalo grass and overrun with bison, antelope, and other wildlife. A few Indians still roamed the grasslands, hunting for hide and food for the reservations to the south, in a territory soon to become Oklahoma.

Abilene lay in that flat country, about halfway between Fort Hays to the west and the small but established settlement of Fort Harker to the east. In 1867, the Pacific and Kansas Railroad extended its track through Abilene and on to the west. As a result, Abilene began to get its share of the traveling population.

Settlers with little or no money homesteaded along the wooded creeks near Abilene and depended on the small stores of goods at Fort Riley, some twenty miles away. There was very little in the way of articles of comfort. The Overland Stage station was built on Mud Creek and tended by a Timothy Hersey. It was later in 1859 in this very cabin that Horace Greeley wrote an article for the *New York Tribune* describing the hazards and ordeals of traveling overland prior to the railroads. Greeley's destination was to be the Pacific, and later when he gave his now-famous advice to "go west young man" he made little mention of the ordeal it might be for one to get there.

There are few records of Virginia and Matthew Loughlin after their arrival in Abilene, but we know that they homesteaded on a strip of land that was bounded on one side by a wide hook in Mud Creek, approximately half the distance from Abilene and Fort Riley. Later, Matthew made several trips to Kansas City to arrange for merchandise to be shipped to Abilene, and with the help of a few stranded cowhands he constructed a small frame building in town to house what was to be his general store, although he held on to his farm.

By about 1867, more than a score of the original settlers had built one-room log cabins along the creek banks. Hersey, who had been one of the first, had asked his wife, a Methodist who possessed a large family Bible, to suggest a name for the settlement. This she found in Luke 3:1, "Tetrarch of Abilene." The town was officially named Abilene late in the year of 1869. At about this time, Joseph G. McCoy, a cattleman from Springfield, Illinois, studied his maps and noted that Abilene was settled along the Pacific and Kansas Railroad. He also noted that the wide Smoky Hill River flowed not far to the south of the settlement. An extension to the Chisholm Trail to the railhead at Abilene would shorten the time for shipping of beef to the eastern markets, he reasoned, and with a more than adequate water supply from the Smoky Hill River plus limitless pasturage of buffalo grass of the plains to feed the cattle waiting for shipment, he started the construction of his stockpens about a mile out of the town.

McCoy's brother and a man by the name of William Suggs were dispatched at the same time to the south into Texas to inform the ranchers of the new market for cattle in Abilene and the pen accommodations for the herds. Buyers of beef farther east from Memphis, St. Louis, Chicago,

Kansas City, and many other cities where the need for beef existed began to arrive in Abilene. During 1869, over 160,000 head of cattle arrived in Abilene, along with cowhands by the hundreds. Texas Street, Abilene's main thoroughfare at the time, became wild with drunken cattle herders and shootouts in as many as ten saloons on the one street. There were four hotels, although only the Drovers Hotel could be classified as such. The Merchants Hotel was third-rate, and the remaining two were referred to as "fancy houses."

James Butler Hickok, a Union scout in the Civil War, became marshal of Abilene for about nine months. Unfortunately, he had less success in keeping Abilene safe than did his predecessor, in spite of many romantic writings of the Wild West that feature his name and reputation.

The early records of Abilene are few, for the bulk of the population was transient. Its population as of April 1871 did not exceed 500 persons, but as of June 1 of that same year, there were 7,000 cowhands eating where they could and, in the main, sleeping under saddle blankets on the open prairie.

Texas cattle virtually put Abilene on the map. Unfortunately for the ranchers and herders, it was not to continue this way. For, in about 1873–1874, only about 120,000 head of cattle were shipped from Abilene to the East, down from a high of 300,000 head that were shipped in the summer of 1870. It was the last of its great cattle days. In the few years during Abilene's history, more than 600,000 head of longhorn cattle were driven up the Chisholm Trail to Abilene's railhead and shipped to the East. In addition, countless numbers of bison were also sent east for food and hides. The small band of original settlers continued to strengthen their roots. Forty-three of the residents, including the Loughlin family, signed a petition on September 3, 1869, and Abilene became a city. Five of the petitioners were appointed to the probate court to act as trustees until an election could be held. The permanent resident population now numbered in the four hundreds.

As the cattle drives became a thing of the past, wheat became known as the future of Kansas. For, at about this same time, a farmer and neighbor of the Loughlins, by the name of Henry, had started sowing his first crops of winter wheat. The Russian Mennonites, who had also settled in this area, introduced a wheat known as "turkey red," and Kansas was beginning to be recognized everywhere as the Wheat State. The grain was selling for $1.15 a bushel, and Henry increased his small area of plantings to 5,000 acres, as did his neighbors. Henry, referred to by then as the "Wheat King," married a local girl and built himself and his bride a palatial residence in Abilene at the northwest corner of 14th and Buckeye. The area's population had stabilized, and the general store, now located on a corner of an important intersection, became the easier of the two lives that the Loughlins had been living. The farm near Mud Creek was sold, and the Loughlins moved into a flat that they had prepared above the store, and there they settled for many years.

The general store changed its merchandise many times in the years that followed, in character with the changing times. Merchandise that was not on display could be ordered by catalog from Chicago or Kansas City and was shipped by train. Machinery for farmers was also ordered in this manner. The store's business grew to a proportion never dreamed of by the venturesome couple.

A storeroom behind the main store was used to house merchandise that became unmarketable; large decorated tin flour canisters that were originally used to hold tea and spices; barrels and kegs that once were filled with flour, sugar, pickles; glass candy jars long emptied of their colorful and sugary display were all lined up on the storeroom's shelves. Candy and coffee eventually became packaged. A big red-and-gold-striped coffee grinder with a huge handwheel was set in a corner next to a balance scale with iron weights. An extra set of tiny brass weights marked for ounces was found close by, but no small scale for their use was visible. A glass-encased stamp scale with its own built-in counterweights was found nearby, reminding one of the time when the general store had also served as a post office.

Piles of furnishings took up over half of the storeroom's area and consisted mainly of chairs, tables, and cast-iron heating stoves. There were one or two woven wicker baby perambulators with extra-large wooden spoked wheels, and there was a large pile of early farmhand tools, such as scythes with wooden cradles to catch the grain as the blade cut with a big semicircular sweep. Plenty of kerosene lamps hung from the rafters, mostly of the variety used in farm work rather than for house lighting or decoration.

The auction that had been set up was to dispose of the objects in the storeroom. Many boxes had not yet been opened. It wasn't a forced sale or an estate sale. It was simply an act of the present store owners to auction things that had filled their only storeroom for years. It was probably the first "garage sale" of its kind, for its contents all predated the day of the automobile.

For the collector of Victorian things, it was a bonanza. Most of the articles were as new as the day they were packed and shipped to the store. There were earlier items as well, for many objects were bartered in exchange for supplies during the days of the cattle drives, and were packed away for posterity. Some of these objects were carried up from the Deep South by ranchers, or left by the people who came to visit them.

Other items belonged to settlers who couldn't make it financially and had to sell back things they couldn't pay for.

The flat above the store, the former living quarters of the Loughlins, had remained as it was furnished many years ago. The new owners of the general store lived elsewhere and were more interested in contemporary furnishings. They had removed none of the Loughlins' effects. There had been no need to. So it remained as it had been, jam-packed with memorabilia of the early days of Abilene.

As retailers in a hectic and transient community, the Loughlins were given ample opportunity to collect those furnishings that struck their fancy. Colorful Amberina glass, blown and elegantly engraved bottles, decanters, and goblets came into their home by way of the back bar of a notorious saloon, to satisfy a food bill. Their better silver objects arrived the same way, having been acquired by the same saloon through the gaming tables. Silver-mounted hand guns were often used in lieu of cash, as were the finer rifles. The pine desk on the maple frame had been bought in Kansas City to be used in the store. It was later moved to their living quarters upstairs. The carved and gilded Empire mirror was a birthday gift to Virginia in 1875, as were the rosewood lady's and gentleman's chairs. Everything there was to be sold.

The auction at Abilene was a rare one, advertised as it was from coast to coast by all the trade publications. It was even publicized in collectors' magazines. Collectors of period pieces were there, as were historians interested in that particular part of the country, and local groups. It is not possible to sit or stand around at an auction for a whole day with your eyes glued to the auctioneer. It wouldn't be any fun if you did. Like many of the collectors that were present, we came from far away and easily fell into the group of optimistic bidders. There is something for everyone at an auction, particularly one like this that had so much to offer. The interest of all these people who had come great distances attests to the value, interest, and fun of attending auctions and building one's own collection. You can always count on each auction being a new and different experience, and on having a wonderful, exciting day.

Top left: Gilt eagle and cornucopia mirror. Circular mirror has acorn motif. (Metropolitan Museum)

Center: Queen Anne mahogany drop-leaf dining table, 1730–1746. This classic dining table was easier to ship on freight wagons because of its drop leaves. The large, rigidly constructed furnishings were more likely to have been made locally.

Top right: Tulip and bull's-eye fleur-de-lis pressed glass goblets. Late Victorian glass was made as far west as Ohio and later in Illinois. The fancy pressed designs were most popular.

Center right: Bird decal on silver-resist pitcher. Late Victorian.

Bottom left: Transfer-printed or decal on copper luster. General Jackson pitcher.

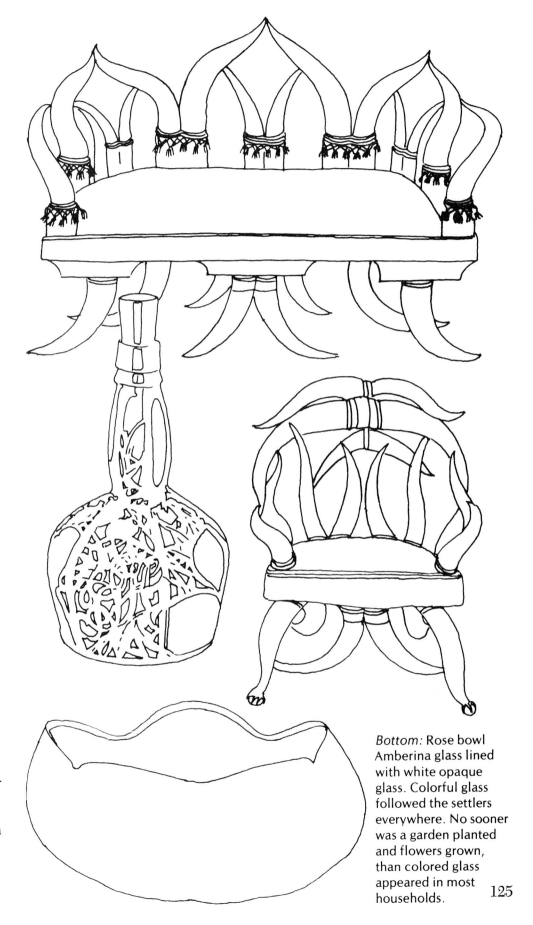

Top and center right: As the West and Southwest gained importance in the great cattle-raising days, furniture-makers created a unique American style. Elk, buffalo, and steer horns combined with leather and fabric upholstery to suit the maker. Theodore Roosevelt, whose hunting prowess was familiar to most, was credited with this original idea, although not a maker. Fad started in middle 1800s and lasted until the turn of the century. These strange furnishings might be said to be a truly American primitive idea, although using horn for furnishings was not totally original. It was as American as an Indian tepee. Those pieces that did last might attribute their longevity to lack of use as well as sturdy construction, for comfort was not a major consideration in the design.

Center left: Silver overlay glass decanter. These popular decanters were used for strong beverages in the better homes. The silver acted not only as a decorative embellishment, but as a reinforcing agent to the glass. Nineteenth century.

Bottom: Rose bowl Amberina glass lined with white opaque glass. Colorful glass followed the settlers everywhere. No sooner was a garden planted and flowers grown, than colored glass appeared in most households.

125

Top: Fine decorations hand-designed and painted on early Dutch chest on table. Drawer is also decorated. Stretchers are interestingly scrolled. (Metropolitan Museum)

Left: Handsome carved mahogany lyre clock with simple acorn finial of the same wood. This fine piece carries no metal or gilding in its decoration. Clocks, of course, followed all but the earliest beginning of every settlement. Not only were they useful and decorative, their appearance in a home was also highly prestigious.

Right: Unusual armchair with round back. Turnings are elegantly designed and are of maple. Connecticut, early eighteenth century. Many individual applications of design were added to a basic Windsor construction, especially during Victorian times.

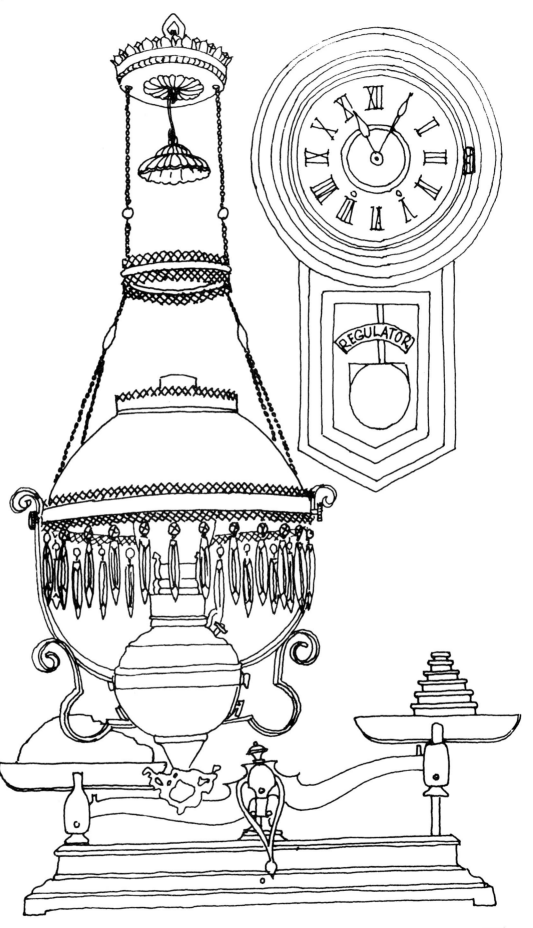

Left: Victorian hanging lamp with plain opaque white shade and stamped brass kerosene font. Girandoles are of pressed glass. The smoke bell is of pressed brass. Spring counterweights make this popular lamp adjustable.

Top right: The wall regulator clock made in Connecticut was a most dependable timepiece. Thousands of these clocks were made throughout the late eighteenth and nineteenth centuries.

Bottom: Cast-iron store balance scale with brass pans. The weights are covered with brass. This inexpensive scale was in use almost everywhere by the middle of the nineteenth century.

Scales such as this balance type came in a variety of sizes and some were designed for special use. The weights were iron or brass and in some cases the polishing of those weights was twice advantageous to the storekeeper, for eventually the burnishing wore away a bit of the weight. We can assume that the brightwork was for cleanliness and not deliberately dishonest.

127

Top left: Mocha pitcher with seaweed decoration. Most of the patterns on mocha-ware appear to be similar to this seaweed motif. However, the colors of the glazes in their beautiful subdued tones make this a most attractive pottery.

Center left: Humped-back six-leg love seat, simulated bamboo, 1775–1800. This is a modification of the basic Windsor design, one of the many variations of the love seat.

Top right: Queen Anne highboy. Mahogany. Early nineteenth century.

Bottom right: Blown, cut, and elaborately engraved bottle. Brilliant faceted stopper. Extravagant copper-wheel engraving of galloping horse and landscape. Late nineteenth century. At that time copper-wheel engraving was most popular, and the artisans who produced the many classic pastoral designs on glass are certainly recognized for their artistic qualities.

Top left: Handsome cast-iron decorated coffee mill for store use. This mill has a brass eagle finial. 1870–1880.

Bottom left: Heavy tin pineapple mold for cakes and puddings. Berks County, Pennsylvania, 1840. Molds made by tinsmiths of this period cover a multiplicity of designs and subjects—fruits, fish, flowers, and simple geometric patterns.

Top right: Brass library table lamps with eight-hour kerosene font. These attractive lamps are often referred to as "student" lamps.

Center right: Pair of blown clear-glass cruets. These are two-piece mold and simulate cut glass facets. New England, nineteenth century.

Bottom right: Hand-use kitchen coffee mill. Cast-iron and walnut box with drawer.

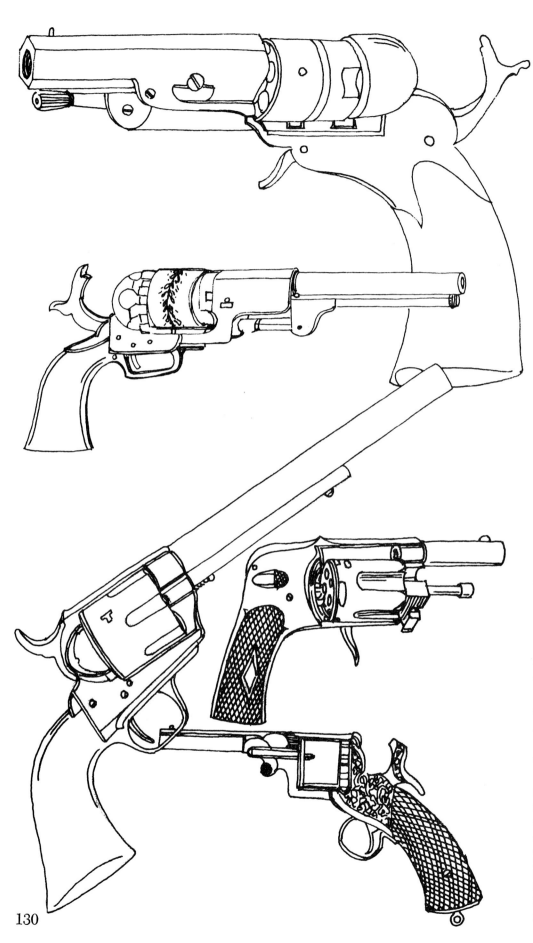

Top: The Colt repeating pistol as advertised in Daggett's *New York City Directory for 1845.* Hyde and Goodriche of New Orleans is listed as one of its preferred dealers. The emperor of Russia, the emperor of Austria, the Imam of Muscat, as well as the Texas army and navy were proud users of this firearm.

Upper left center: This holster weapon invented by Sam Colt in 1836 truly was the "gun that won the West."

Lower left center: Another long-barreled Colt.

Lower right center: This European revolver was found in large supply in the Southwest. Cylinder can be swung out for loading.

Bottom right: Webley's revolver with chase work on the metal areas.

The hand gun (or holster pistol) was a way of life in most of the West of that time. Freely advertised and easily purchased, no self-respecting cowhand would be without one. Long after the Indians were on their reservations and some semblance of law and order was apparent in most settlements, the pistol was still a basic part of the cowhand's equipment, even if there was little need for its use.

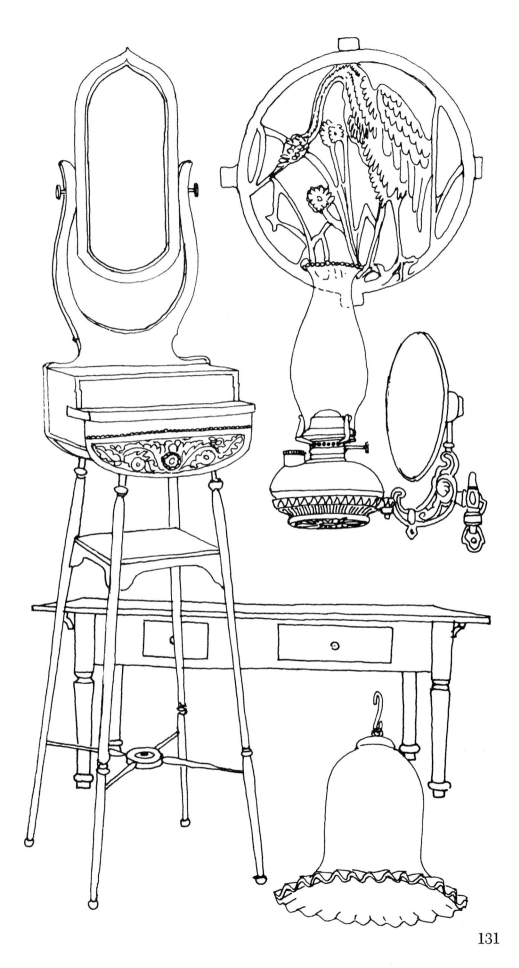

Left: Shaving stand, late Victorian. Adjustable mirror and single drawer. Walnut. About 1880. Obviously this is for the man who stands while shaving.

Top right: Cast-iron trivet of unusual bird design. Collectors of these Victorian pieces have numbered the designs in the hundreds. Original castings can usually be identified by the fine work in the design; recasting thickens the finer metal work and is easily detected.

Upper right center: Cast-iron wall-bracket lamp with mercury glass reflector, brass burner fittings. The mercury reflector multiplies the candle-power many times and was a most important addition to a lamp.

Lower right center: Pennsylvania Dutch table with removable top and freestanding legs. This characteristic farm table is typical of the Dutch saying: "Built not for pretty but hell for strong."

Bottom right: Milk glass smoke bell to hang over lamp chimney to catch smoke and keep ceiling clean. These attractive and utilitarian pieces were made in all shapes, colors, and varieties of glass and metal.

Top right: Early-eighteenth-century pine desk with maple frame, typical of hand-molding plane work. Fine turnings and stretcher construction. The design appears to have several influences, Dutch and English, although it undoubtedly is an American piece.

Center left: Late Victorian wall bracket lamp with pressed glass font and shade. This design was continued long after gas replaced kerosene. It is noteworthy that as these wall lamps were manufactured in Victorian times, the efficient mercury reflector disappeared.

Bottom left: Carved and gilded Empire mirror with half-spindle decorations. This popular mirror was made in quantity during Victorian times. Later the half-spindles were coated with a plaster undersurface.

Bottom right: Earthenware pitcher made in Cincinnati, Ohio, is one of the items marking the beginning of contemporary artware, 1883. This particular shape is reminiscent of Greek urns.

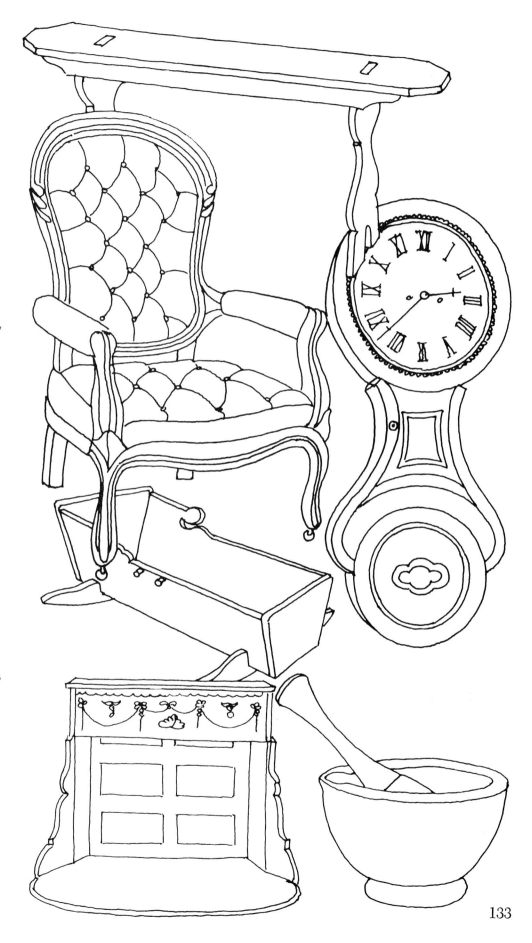

Top: Scrolled-leg trestle stool. Legs are mortised through top plank. When designed for porch, legs were scrolled only on front edge. (Authors' collection)

Upper left center: Victorian gentleman's chair. Armchair has low upholstered arms. Typical of American factory-made furnishings between 1860–1875.

Lower left center: Child's pine cradle, 1800.

Bottom left: The Franklin stove, invented in 1742 by Benjamin Franklin, saved much wood and produced more efficient heating. Literally a stove lining for the fireplace, it was able to rid a room of smoke and soot. Made in standard parts, it was a forerunner of the iron stove.

Center right: Wall regulator clock with striking banjo movement. George D. Hatch, North Attleboro, Massachusetts, 1850.

Bottom right: Granite mortar and pestle. Pharmacist pulverizer.

133

Top left: Large free-blown drinking glass with steeple design and polychromed enamel decoration.

Bottom left: Walnut chair patterned after the popular balloon-back form, Victorian, and an extremely popular basic design. These were made as ladies', gentlemen's, and general use chairs. Mahogany, rosewood, and maple were as popular as walnut although more expensive.

Top right and bottom right: Free-blown decanters with star, mushroom, and clear stoppers. New England, 1770s.

134

The House on
Russian Hill in
San Francisco

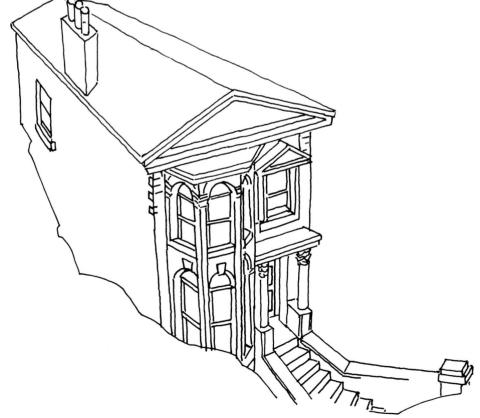

In the city of San Francisco, exciting new architectural structures are being built, and areas are being renovated. Most of the handsome, modern buildings are confined to the main business areas. Fortunately, at the same time attention has been given to preserving some of the architectural originals that gave this lovely city its unique look.

San Francisco is most attractively placed on a group of hills and is almost completely surrounded by water. Its geography is reminiscent of European cities, such as Lisbon and Rome. Its unique construction of houses placed on steep inclines of streets is not to be seen elsewhere in the United States, and probably had much to do with the architectural character of the dwellings, as did the winter winds and rains from the Pacific Ocean. The heavy timber construction of earlier houses has the feel of the sea, as if built by ships' carpenters. The decorative wood façades give one the feeling of sturdy and highly ornamental galleons.

At the time that early Victorianism settled in along the Atlantic seaboard, San Francisco was but a tiny and little known settlement on the far Pacific coast. Not until 1848–1849, the years of the gold rush, did San Francisco become known everywhere in the world. During those hectic two years, this settlement of not more than two thousand hardy souls suddenly swelled to an unmanageable twenty-five thousand. Along with its cataclysmic population change, came an instant need for services and people to perform them. Goods were needed to satisfy the demands of housing, eating, transportation, clothing, and health. All of these essentials had to be brought in or developed within the community.

The demands were little different from those of any other growing community, except that in San Francisco everything happened faster.

Gold attracted people from many walks of life other than those of settling, farming, and building a stable, cohesive society.

It is difficult to believe that in 1769, less than one hundred years before the gold rush, San Francisco was a barren, treeless wilderness, swept by Pacific winds and surrounded by shallow salt-marsh inlets. It was to this desolate scene that forty-seven footweary Spanish soldiers led by a Captain Gaspar de Portolá came. Sighting what would later be known as the San Francisco Bay area, Captain de Portolá's expedition started out to explore and map Monterey Bay, an inlet from the Pacific, some sixty miles to the south. The group apparently bypassed their proper target as ordered and continued to march north for two more days, suddenly coming upon the huge bay with its magnificent and heretofore unknown harbor.

De Portolá's accidental discovery was infinitely more important than his original assignment. The deep-water entrance to the larger bay would make an impressive harbor for Spanish ships. A small settlement was established to care for the trade that ships would bring to it from all over the world.

Colonizing in that area of the world was not usually undertaken by the Spanish. However, missionaries built a string of primitive but beautiful missions along the desert valleys of Southern California. Constructed of adobe and local woods, these structures were a continuation of the missions found to the south in Mexico. The missions and their tiny aprons of villages were to exert an influence on the artistic and living habits of Californians for many years to come. The small churches are a heritage that has survived all change.

Some twenty years after Mexico freed itself from Spain, California became a territorial part of the United States. Originally peopled by Spaniards, Mexicans, and Indians, few changes had occurred until then. Suddenly the entire bay area of San Francisco was projected into a new age: There was a rush of people from Boston, New York, Philadelphia, and other places on the eastern and southern coasts of the United States, all with new ideas.

To understand the extreme isolation of the Pacific area, one should realize that until almost a decade after the gold rush, San Francisco was still twenty-five days' travel by stagecoach from the Mississippi River. And, it took eighty days to sail around Cape Horn to New York. Until the completion of the Pacific Railroad in 1869 there was little communication with the Atlantic coast.

With the advent of the railroad, a second tidal wave of people descended upon the West Coast. Some 600,000 people made their way to California, and primarily to the same areas that were recovering from the 1848–1849 deluge. These immigrants, however, did not come for the thrill of finding gold, only to return to their places of origin; they came to stay. They came to settle, to trade, to farm, to build, and to manufacture goods. They brought with them most of their worldly wealth and ideas, settling the area with a truly cosmopolitan air.

The pattern of colonization resembled movements to the West. Forty percent of the colonizers were from the Northeast, mainly New England, New York, and Pennsylvania. About 30 percent more came from the Ohio and Illinois valleys. In addition, another 20 percent is said to have come from the South. We can safely assume, by the study of some of the architectural details of the houses, as well as of the furnishings, that some of those who populated the new Pacific area were surely from the gulf coast.

With knowledge of its origins, it is not difficult for one to understand how such a wealth of Victorian antiques accumulated in San Francisco some three thousand miles away from where one would ordinarily expect to find them. Many people at that time could afford to bring many of the material comforts that earlier settlers would have had to leave behind. The railroad made almost all possessions retrievable. There are early accounts of prefabricated houses of timber that were constructed in the East and shipped in sections around Cape Horn, to be assembled upon arriving at their destination. And, in one of the early houses in the city, a front reception hall contained a mirror fourteen feet in length, which was transported around Cape Horn from England. Great cases of porcelain, glass lamps, and furnishings found their way from New Orleans, Galveston, and other southern ports where ships embarked on their way to San Francisco.

The house on Russian Hill was one of the early homes on the hill. It seemed small compared with the neighboring houses that were built later. Styles and neighborhoods change, and the house did not retain its original look. As fashions in architecture changed, the front of the house also changed. Only the basic structure retained its original form. Eventually, the entire front of the house sported a combination of late Victorian architectural forms.

The house was built by a man who had been educated and raised in the East, near Philadelphia, and the house had the appearance of that geographic area. The builder, attracted by the search for gold, finally settled on the beautiful hill overlooking the bay area, surrounding himself with much of the memorabilia of his youth. Furnishings were originally transported by ship from his home in the East, and later moved by train.

A maple desk his father had used in the house in Philadelphia was now in place in its new home on the West Coast. It was a most practical furnishing for the day-to-day business of the San Francisco house. The collection of glass shipped west from Pennsylvania had been his mother's and included pressed, overlay, and some free-blown glass pieces of New England origin. They, too, graced the living room on Russian Hill. The lyre table and the equally unusual Chippendale carved eagle console table with the black marble top had been shipped west by sea and had survived the long journey around Cape Horn in perfect condition. Both of these rare pieces had been a gift to his mother from her sister in Germantown, Pennsylvania. The lyre table was placed between two front windows, below an elegant Hepplewhite filigree mirror. The total arrangement of that front room was an attempt to duplicate the living room he loved and remembered so well as a child in Philadelphia. It all was much the same as he recalled, except for the view from the windows of the blue water of San Francisco Bay far below.

The earthquake and fire were financially disastrous to his business, but his home on the hill and its contents survived intact. The construction of veneer brick over heavy timber was probably one reason so many structures survived the fire and earthquake of 1906.

The gentleman, well along in years and unable to recoup his business losses after the disasters, was compelled to sell some of his prized possessions. In the fall of 1910, he passed away, and his collection of furnishings went on to his family. The rooms, which were filled with memorabilia, were still basically intact, and his family had inherited his interest and love for the antiques. They, in turn, continued to add antiques that they fancied. So the already large collection continued to grow through the First World War. As is usual, pieces were broken from time to time, and part of the collection was sold as decorating fashions changed. Basically, though, the house and its contents remained almost entirely intact, its rooms filled with ornate and overstuffed furnishings so typical of their time. Colorful glass and highly ornamental bric-a-brac, all perfectly comfortable together, survived in truly authentic early and late Victorian settings.

Correct in every detail of the decorator's traditions, packed with objects of Americana from almost everywhere in the United States, this was a most unusual house. When the house was opened to public viewing, most of the lovely objects had been carefully allowed to remain where they had been originally placed in the house by the owner many years before, until the final offering at auction.

Top left: Boat-shaped compote blown into mold with cut design. Conventional tulip pattern interspersed with diamond-filled arches. Strong clear-glass pedestal. Early nineteenth century.

Center left and top right: Two pressed-glass goblets. The familiar sawtooth pattern and New England pine-apple.

Bottom left: Scrolled maple desk on separate frame. Unusual design shows extremely small ball feet. Back feet are duck. This individual design carries no maker's name, but is apparently a very early piece, 1730–1760.

Center right: Sugar bowl and cover, blown from clear lead glass. The oblong shape is reminiscent of Staffordshire earthenware of the same period. New England Glass Company, early 1800s.

Bottom right: Unusual, tall free-blown wineglass in aquamarine nonlead glass, air-twisted stem. Early nineteenth century.

Top left: Pelican savings bank. A mocking cashier's face appears when the coin is deposited. In 1878 this mechanical bank sold for one dollar.

Bottom left: Folding-top table. Duncan Phyfe. Top and frame of fine grain veneer. Base and legs carved of solid mahogany, fine carved eagle pedestal. Empire, 1800–1840.

Top right: Tall clock or grandfather clock by Aaron Willard, 1800. These popular and beautiful clocks are held preciously by the few collectors who are fortunate enough to own one.

Bottom right: Small pitcher, free-blown clear glass. Applied-petal foot, pinched lip. Applied petals of crimping on rigaree. Midwestern, 1850.

143

Top left: Blown celery glass. Clear lead glass, notched rim. Northeastern glass-makers, many of whom were responsible for these fine, blown, cut, and engraved pieces. Pre-Civil War, 1835–1850.

Bottom left: Half-turn gold-leaf mirror with historical painting on top frame of glass. Empire.

Center: Small free-blown vase. Aqua-marine-blue, nonlead glass, characteristic of the Red Wood Glass Works, Watertown, New York. Early nineteenth century.

Top right: Mahogany piecrust tip-top table. Philadelphia, late eighteenth century.

Center right: Lyre-back chair was one of Duncan Phyfe's most popular and original designs.

Bottom right: Mocha-ware pitcher. Bandings of cat's eyes and serpentine ropes. A soft-paste porcelain imported from England.

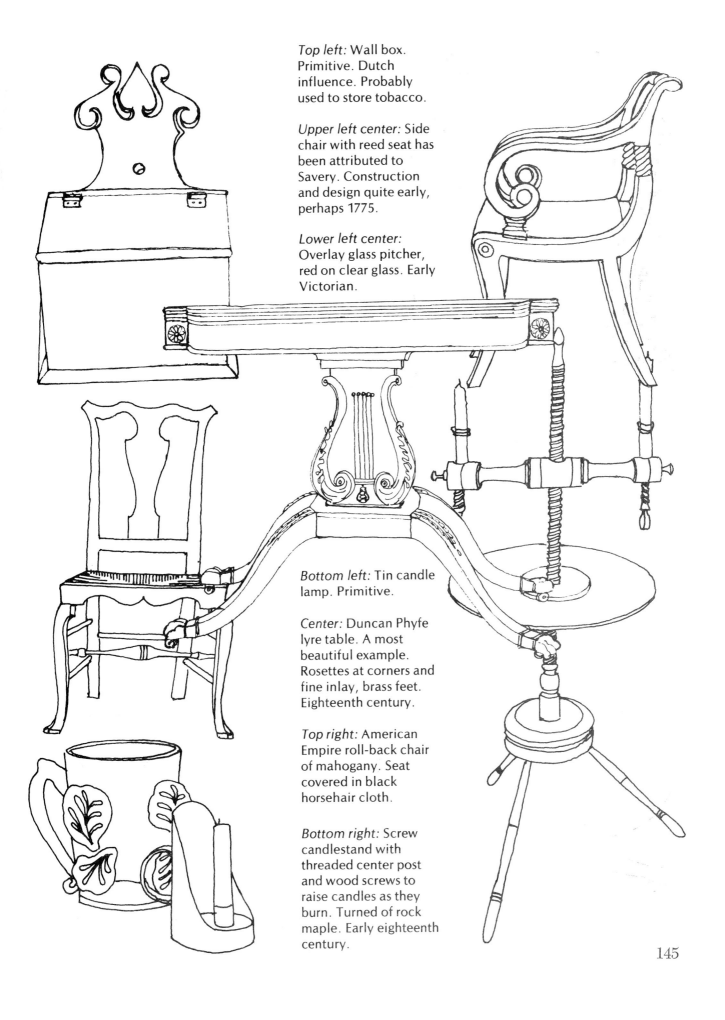

Top left: Wall box. Primitive. Dutch influence. Probably used to store tobacco.

Upper left center: Side chair with reed seat has been attributed to Savery. Construction and design quite early, perhaps 1775.

Lower left center: Overlay glass pitcher, red on clear glass. Early Victorian.

Bottom left: Tin candle lamp. Primitive.

Center: Duncan Phyfe lyre table. A most beautiful example. Rosettes at corners and fine inlay, brass feet. Eighteenth century.

Top right: American Empire roll-back chair of mahogany. Seat covered in black horsehair cloth.

Bottom right: Screw candlestand with threaded center post and wood screws to raise candles as they burn. Turned of rock maple. Early eighteenth century.

145

Top left: Black iron clock set on black marble. Late Victorian. Said to have been made by Ingraham.

Center left: Tiffany table lamp, rough opaque glass shade, base of bronze.

Top right: Sparking lamp, 3″ high. Clear lead glass blown. Single-tube tin burner set in wood plug. Probably from New England, 1820.

Center right: Late Victorian upholstered chair, carved cherry frame. These chairs were made in quantity. One of the many Grand Rapids Furniture Company designs.

Bottom: Empire dining table, wide mahogany boards. Drop leaf can be supported by gate legs. Supporting legs are formed to imitate the bamboo look, a style just then gaining in popularity. 1810.

146

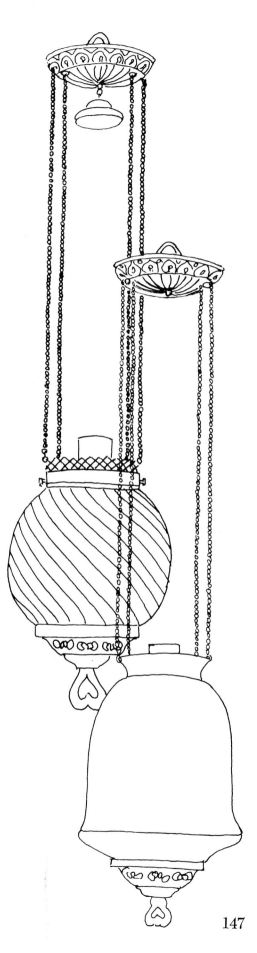

Top left: Tufted lady's chair, typical of American manufacture for mass production in Victorian times. 1860–1875.

Bottom left: Fine Hepplewhite filigree mirror. 1780–1790. Mirrors, both ornamental and framed with a simple molding, rapidly became an important household essential as they were made available. The marketplace grew so rapidly that manufacturers didn't always use care with the silvering of the glass or the design of the frame, and many of these early furnishings disappeared.

Right: Adjustable hanging lamps. Globes are of blown ruby glass and spiral opal glass. Fittings of brass. These Victorian lamps burn kerosene and are usually designed for the high ceiling of the hall area of a house.

147

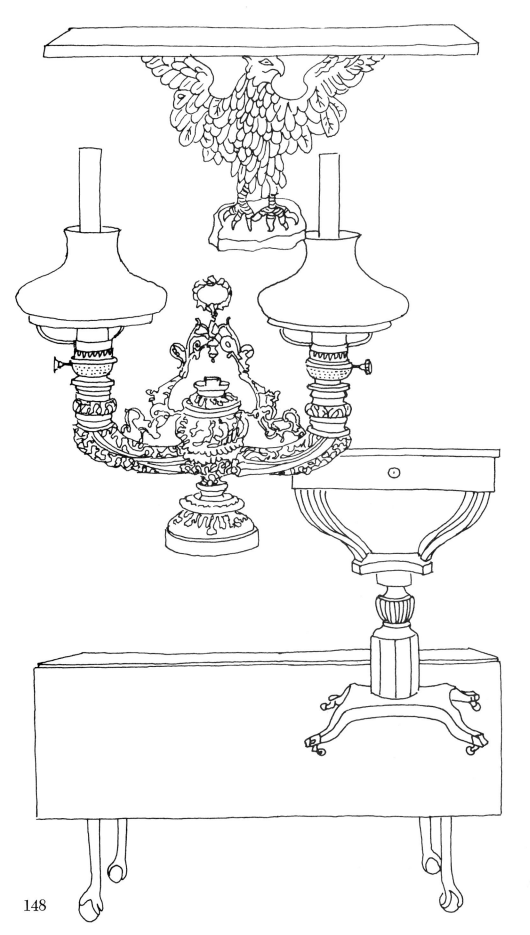

Top: Chippendale carved-pine eagle console. Oblong black marble top above a fluted apron resting on a powerfully carved spread eagle perched on a grassy base. Height 34″, length 5′.

Left: Double student lamp, silver plate with opaque shades. Late 1800s.

Right: Empire table, veneered mahogany. 1800–1820. This small occasional table was one of many designs that fitted into well-furnished early Victorian homes.

Bottom: Chippendale drop leaf, ball-and-claw foot. Walnut, probably from Pennsylvania, 1780–1800. Simple classic design with a one-board leaf. The width of the board designated the depth of the drop leaf, for "good" tables were almost never made of top boards put together to make them wide.

Top left: Two pressed-glass bottles. Nonlead glass, probably Pittsburgh-Monongahela glass houses, 1820–1830.

Top right: Stiegel-type flint-paneled vase. This early piece of American glass can be seen at the Brooklyn Museum.

Center: Wrought-iron andirons. This late Victorian ironwork was advertised in a catalog by A. Kimbel & Sons, New York City, 1880.

Bottom left: Fine Burmeseware or Pomona vase with etched-flower design attributed to New England Glass Company, 1875.

Bottom right: Gothic church chair (or cathedra) was distinctly Romanesque. Designed by Richardson for the Church of the Unity, Springfield, Massachusetts. Late eighteenth century.

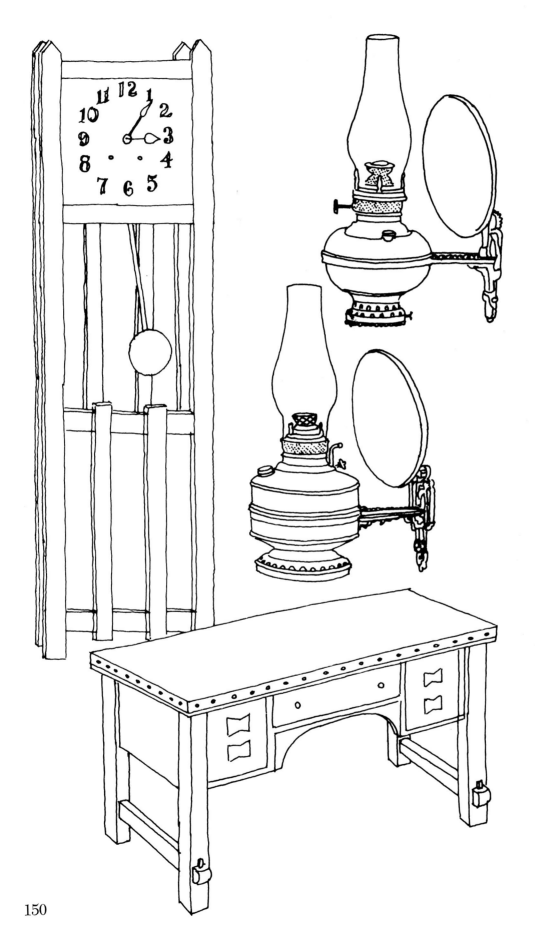

Left: Mission-style
standing clock.

Right: Two wall-bracket
lamps of the late
nineteenth century.
Made in mass pro-
duction and sold by
catalog as well as at
most general stores.
The mercury reflectors
are an added value.

Bottom: Leather-
topped Mission desk.

The late Victorian
and turn-of-the-century
material on this page is
a tribute to those who
prefer to build things
strong. Gustav Stickley,
1857–1942, exemplifies
this attribute with his
Mission or Craftsman
furniture. Stickley, who
was influenced by the
Shakers, rebelled
against the era of
marble tops and fabric
upholstery. Made in the
north-central part of
the United States, these
period pieces survived
time by their
indestructible design.

Top: Walnut desk box with brass fittings. Early eighteenth century. These desk boxes were placed on tables and were the forerunners of the desk, later to be built with supporting legs of their own.

Center left: "Lady's companion" lifting top. Extremely interesting pattern, solid mahogany. 1820–1840.

Center: Fine tumbler blown of clear lead glass. Straight-side form with heavy base. Copper-wheel engraving, said to have been decorated by an engraver employed by Burger and Sons Glassworks, Philadelphia.

Center right: Small tumbler blown of clear flint glass, three-piece mold. Circa, 1830.

Bottom: Classic Hepplewhite inlaid mahogany sideboard with reeded legs. This is an extremely fine piece. Its simplicity makes it much prized.

151

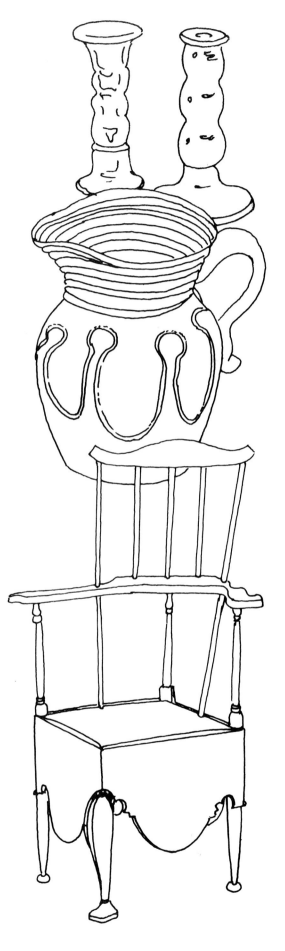

Top left: Corner frame with cupboard on top. Early eighteenth century. (Metropolitan Museum)

Bottom left: Two lamp screens. *Right,* seventeenth or eighteenth century, pine, primitive. *Left,* equally early but more elegant, with fine floral display.

Top right: Free-blown glass candlestick from clear-red amber glass. Nonlead. Miniature glass candlestick, free-blown of deep-green glass. Products of a glass house in Stoddard, New Hampshire, 1840–1860.

Center right: Lily-pad pitcher, free-blown glass characteristic of a New York glass house. 1830–1860.

Bottom right: Corner chair, comb-back style and Windsor influenced. Early eighteenth century. (Metropolitan Museum)

Index

160